Case Studies in
Public Services Management

Case Studies in Public Services Management

Edited by
Alan Lawton and David McKevitt

Copyright © Blackwell Publishers Ltd, 1996

First published 1996
2 4 6 8 10 9 7 5 3 1

Blackwell Publishers Ltd
108 Cowley Road
Oxford OX4 1JF
UK

Blackwell Publishers Inc.
238 Main Street
Cambridge, Massachusetts 02142
USA

British Library Cataloguing in Publication Data
A CIP catalogue record for this book is available from the British Library.

Library of Congress Cataloging-in-Publication Data
Case studies in public services management / edited by Alan Lawton and
David McKevitt.
p.   cm.
Includes bibliographical references and index.
ISBN 0–631–19579–3 (pbk. :–alk. paper)
1. Public administration—Case studies.   I. Lawton, Alan.
II. McKevitt, David.
JF1351.C354   1996
350—dc20   95–22604
CIP

Typeset in 11 on 13 pt Ehrhardt
by Graphicraft Typesetters Ltd, Hong Kong

This book is printed on acid-free paper.

Contents

List of Figures   vii

List of Tables   viii

List of Contributors   ix

Introduction   1

1   The Vision and Reality of an Executive Agency   6
    Charles Ferguson and Deirdre McGill

2   Strategic Change at Kirby College   32
    Julie Rayner

3   Strategic Change in Local Government Management:
    Comparative Case Studies   57
    Alan Lawton and David McKevitt

4   Light at the End of the Tunnel   73
    Paul Ketchley and Pierre Mongin

5   Merging into Ribbon   90
    Mike Dempsey

6   The Metropolitan Police Plus Programme   103
    Garry Elliot

7   Implementing Community Care   123
    Alan Lawton

8   Wellcare Hospital Trust
    Alan Lawton and David McKevitt   148

9   Networking in Wales: European Regional Development
    Fund and Welsh Office – Local Authority Relations   158
    Russell Deacon and Alan Lawton

10 Local Authority Decision Making: The Traders of the
    Uffizi Gallery in Florence   168
    Chiara Narcisi

11 Capital Accounting Case Study: UK Local Government   184
    Geoff Jones

Index   205

Figures

1.1   Agency Management Board   24
5.1   Stakeholder map of Ribbon   98
6.1   Offences and clear-ups in the Metropolitan Police
      Division – 1939–1989   106
6.2   Metropolitan Police area structure   116
6.3   Senior management structure of the Metropolitan Police
      in 1989   118

Tables

I.1   Case studies and issues raised   5
1.1   Service targets and performance   26–27
1.2   Efficiency and performance   27
2.1   Council-funded provision in further education colleges   53
2.2   Enrolments in colleges (full time)   53
2.3   Enrolments in colleges (part time)   54
2.4   Higher education provision in further education colleges
      franchised from higher education institutions   54
5.1   The organizational combination process   91
6.1   Summary of functional cost information   119
6.2   'Taking everything into account, would you say that the
      police in this area do a good job or a poor job?'   119
6.3   'How safe do you feel walking alone in this area after dark?'   120
6.4   'What do you feel are the most important problems in this
      area that the police should concentrate their efforts on?'   120
6.5   'In what ways, if any, do you think that the police could
      help the public safeguard their own property from theft?'   121
6.6   Policing priorities – tasks   121
6.7   Policing priorities – offences   122
7.1   Expenditure by client group 1994–1995   141
7.2   Expenditure on elderly 1994–1995   142
7.3   Expenditure on people with physical disabilities 1994–1995   142
7.4   Expenditure on mental health and illness 1994–1995   142
7.5   Expenditure on people with learning disabilities 1994–1995   143
7.6   Stourvale social services departments   143
7.7   Private sector and voluntary establishments   143
7.8   Location of social services deparements' establishments   144
7.9   People aged 65 years and above by district   145

Contributors

Russell Deacon, Cardiff Institute of Higher Education
Mike Dempsey, Unison
Garry Elliot, Metropolitan Police
Charles Ferguson, Ulster Business School
Geoff Jones, Open University Business School
Paul Ketchley, London Ambulance Service
Alan Lawton, Open University Business School
Deirdre McGill, Northern Ireland Social Security Agency
David McKevitt, University of Limerick
Pierre Mongin, Centre National de la Fonction Publique Teratoriale, Lille
Chiara Narcisi, University of Florence
Julie Rayner, Middlesbrough College

Introduction

The use of case studies is recognized as an important part of management education. American business schools have a long tradition of using case studies to teach business policy, marketing, finance and organizational development. In recent years European business schools have made increasing use of case studies in their teaching. Similarly, training managers and independent consultants now use case studies for management development and in company training programmes. However, many of the case studies have been developed for use by business studies students and managers working in the private sector. While many of these cases may be applied to public and voluntary sector organizations, such cases rarely capture the distinctiveness of the public sector. There are, of course, many similarities between organizations working in different sectors and the management task can be the same. However, the changing context of the political environment, the ambiguity of goals, the challenge of managing a multiplicity of different stakeholders and the traditions and ethos of public service provide a distinctive management context. The case studies in this book address the complexities and challenges of managing in the public services.

Many of the developed countries are faced with similar problems and are choosing similar solutions to those problems. What should be the size of the core public service be? How can it be funded? How can service to the citizen be improved? What are the appropriate management skills required to ensure the delivery of effective services? In response, public sector organizations around the world are adopting private sector approaches, changing their organizational structures, rethinking the role of central agencies and seeking to develop new ways of delivering their services. The UK public sector is not unique in undergoing profound changes in recent years. The local government manager in the UK, for example, will appreciate the need to satisfy the multiplicity of stakeholders that were involved in the decision-making process illustrated in the case study of Florentine street traders.

The book is aimed at final-year undergraduates and postgraduates studying public sector management and managers in public services organizations.

What is a Case Study?

A case study is a vehicle for learning about management issues. It provides a simulated management situation through which theoretical concepts and approaches can be applied and their feasibility and suitability assessed, thereby providing greater insights into management issues. The case study approach seeks to identify issues, analyse problems, develop solutions to these problems and to assess implementation challenges arising from these solutions. The case study method is based on real-life practical problems and as such seeks to make the issues come alive for the student.

Case studies vary considerably in length, in the amount of information contained, in the number of issues raised and in the way they are taught. Sometimes the problem for analysis is clear and sometimes it has to be dug out of a wealth of information, often conflicting. A case study rarely contains all the information that one would like. However, managers are rarely in a position to make decisions with complete information. Managers make assumptions where information is incomplete, but taking care to justify these assumptions.

Case studies rarely have right or wrong answers; answers may be more or less appropriate depending on the strength of the supporting arguments and the use that is made of the available information. Sometimes that information is in the form of financial data, data about customers or in the form of opinions expressed by different stakeholders. The student needs to assess the validity of the different kinds of information and the weight to be given to it. All this can, of course, be very frustrating, but managing involves making decisions with limited information, limited time and limited resources.

Skills Developed by Case Study Method

Case analysis promotes the discussion of organizational problems and as such is problem-oriented rather than concerned with the acquisition of knowledge. The case study is concerned with practice: what are the problems of the organization and how can these be solved? Theory can provide a framework against which solutions can be tested. Case studies may be designed to develop:

- *comprehension*   students need to grasp the detail of the case, often in a limited space of time, and to differentiate between relevant and irrelevant information;
- *analysis*   students need to break the case study into its constituent parts and examine the relationship between them;
- *problem diagnosis*   often it is unclear what the problem is and why, for example, an organization is not performing as well as expected;
- *problem solution*   case studies often require the generation and evaluation of different options. A key question is often 'what would happen if X did this'?;
- *application of theory*   often a case involves the application of general managerial concepts or theory to a specific example;
- *use of quantitative tools*   a case may allow the application of quantitative data so that students can understand how data can be used;
- *presentation skills*   an important part of a case study may be the presentation of findings either orally or in the form of a written report. A key management skill is communication and the suitability, feasibility and acceptability of solutions may be tested;
- *inter-group communication*   it is very rare that managers work in isolation and most managers work in teams for at least part of their time. The case study method can help develop skills required for working in groups. A good case will generate discussion, allow the student to form opinions and provide the material to defend those opinions. During discussion new insights are likely to emerge: as we indicated above, there are usually no right or wrong answers to case studies.

How to Analyse Cases

It is important that, in the first instance, students read the case and understand some of the issues. It may be appropriate to read the case quickly to arrive at an overview and then to analyse the different dimensions. This could be done in subgroups where each subgroup examines a particular issue before reporting back to the main group. Typically cases might be broken down into issues covering finance, external environment, structure, people, processes and so on. It is important, however, that in subdividing the case students do not lose sight of the overall picture.

The case will pose a number of problems that need addressing and students will need to identify major and minor problems and prioritize their importance. Alternative solutions may be generated and evaluated. Typically, cases require a decision and an implementation plan involving short-term, medium-term and long-term solutions. Solutions will be tested against the context of the case, the appropriateness of the organizational structures and processes, and the challenges of the wider environment.

It may be appropriate that students adopt particular roles in seeking to understand the feelings, opinions and values of key stakeholders. Such role playing can lead to very lively discussions. However, care needs to be taken that students do not overstep the mark and that they respect the opinions and feelings of others. A case is there to simulate real life and, most importantly, to provide a learning opportunity for students. Where role playing is used it is important that students do 'come out' of role and reflect on the management lessons learned.

About the Cases in this Book

The cases are written by a mixture of academics and practitioners. This is consistent with our belief that the use of case studies allows the practical examination of theoretical issues. The cases vary in length and in complexity and in the amount of information contained. Our aim is to raise many of the current issues that confront public services managers in a variety of organizations both in the UK and elsewhere. Table I.1 offers a guide to the issues raised and the focus of attention in each of the case studies.

Table I.1 Case studies and issues raised

Case	Issues raised
1 Executive agency	Role of Next Steps Agencies, accountability, performance measurement, change
2 Kirby College	Competition in Further Education, changing cultures, strategy formulation
3 Strategic change in local government	Strategy formulation and implementation, comparative management
4 Light at the End of the Tunnel	Comparative management, changing structures in local government
5 Trade union merger	Changing culture, organizational mergers
6 The Metropolitan Police	Changing culture, competing organizational objectives
7 Community care	Implementation issues, managing across organizational and professional boundaries
8 National Health Service Trust	Performance measurement, changing context of health service delivery
9 European Regional Development Fund in Wales	Centre–local relations, networking and partnerships
10 Uffizi Museum, Florence	Local government decision making, managing stakeholders
11 Capital accounting	Role of professionals, values in accounting, stakeholder analysis

1

The Vision and Reality of an Executive Agency

CHARLES FERGUSON AND DEIRDRE MCGILL

In his opening remarks at the launch of the Social Security Agency (NI) in July 1991, the Chief Executive set out his vision for its future:

> My aim is for the Agency to become renowned for the quality of its products and its service; and to be a by-word for efficiency and value for money. I want its staff to be committed to the principles and aims of the Agency; and to be acclaimed experts in their field. I want them to be excited by the prospect of taking on new responsibilities; to be enthusiastic about their job; and to be proud to tell their friends, as I am, that they work in the Social Security Agency.

These sentiments reflect more than a personal vision by the Chief Executive. He is echoing the principles laid down in the *Treasury and Civil Service Committee 7th Report, The Next Steps Initiative,* 1991 which – building on the Financial Management Initiative (FMI) – aimed to introduce far-reaching reforms within the Civil Service that would bring about a sustained pressure for improving the delivery of services to the public and to Ministers and for achieving better value for money (see Appendix 1.1, 'The Vision for Agencies').

This case examines three major issues arising from the introduction of Next Steps agencies:

1 The tension between the agency and its parent department over the location of accountability.
2 The requirement to move to a performance-based culture.
3 The implications for human resource strategies.

The Social Security Agency (Northern Ireland)

The Social Security Agency (SSA) was launched in Northern Ireland in July 1991. Previously all policy and operational matters relating to social security in Northern Ireland were dealt with under the umbrella of the Department of Health and Social Services (DHSS). The SSA is the largest executive agency in the Northern Ireland Civil Service (NICS) and the seventh largest in the UK. Employing over 5,500 staff in a network of offices throughout the Province, the SSA is responsible for the administration of benefits worth £2,000 million annually.

The context within which the SSA operates is unique in a number of respects. The SSA has to deal with particularly high levels of unemployment and associated requests for help arising from the social deprivation which has been emphasized by the spiralling poverty and violence of the last quarter of a century. It had to respond to damage to its buildings through the terrorist bombing campaign, intimidation threats from paramilitaries on its members and individual personal attacks on its staff. As one senior member of the Agency put it:

> Our business can be described as 'peddling poverty' and staff can as a result be the recipients of frustrated members of the public who associate the disallowance of their payment of benefit with the individual concerned, without a real understanding that they can only act within the legislation.

Although a demand-led business, the SSA has to bid for its resources within the 'block allocation system', which is the unique format for resource allocation of central government funds to Northern Ireland. This means that the Secretary of State for Northern Ireland has discretion to allocate resources between all Northern Ireland departments and agencies, and therefore the Northern Ireland block resources are subject to the pressures arising from all departments and agencies. Due to competing social factors there are often conflicting pressures arising within this block system, for instance whether to place priority on employment, training, security and so on. The SSA has to be responsive to fluctuating demands in claims for benefit and to changes in policy and legislation, yet must compete equally with other priority policy and security issues.

In practice this means the SSA can bid for more money in-year to meet unforseen demand or, alternatively, it may have to surrender money to meet the priority needs of other government departments within the block allocation system. Consequently the SSA, through the DHSS, has less management flexibility than its Whitehall counterparts. For instance, its sister agency, the Benefits Agency, deals direct with Treasury. The reality of working within the block allocation system has been neatly summarized by a senior member of the Agency: 'Working within the "block system" is a very uncertain and imprecise business. This lack of certainty about budgets can sometimes affect planning, and ultimately the quality of the service offered by the SSA.'

The SSA is involved exclusively in the administration of social security. Social security is a very unified business which has only two real activities: the administration of benefits and contributions. There is, therefore, virtually no opportunity to generate income and the SSA currently operates as a 'gross running cost' regime with all monies required to administer its business being voted through Parliament.

The limitations within which the SSA operates are well articulated by its Chief Executive:

> Running an Agency as far as possible on business lines is, of course, an important tenet of Next Steps theology. I say 'as far as possible', because there are limitations to how far we, in particular, can model ourselves on the commercial world. We cannot, for example, diversify into new product lines of our own choosing or decide to stop paying certain benefits or leave parts of Northern Ireland unserviced, just because the administration cost is too high. Nor can we pull down the shutters and serve only a certain number of customers if we're short of money. Instead we are obligated to run whatever benefit schemes the Government decides to introduce, deal with every single demand no matter how complex or how long it may take to clear and we must cover all areas of the Province whatever the cost.

The SSA took an early decision to put in place a new organizational structure. A six-member board comprising the Chief Executive and five directors was established to manage the Agency and to enhance the effective delivery of services. Two of the directors maintain responsibility for all operational matters, while the remainder are charged with specialist responsibilities in the areas of strategic and business planning, human resource management and financial management. The main managerial elements of this new structure are outlined in Appendix 1.2.

In keeping with all agencies, the SSA's terms of reference are set down in the Social Security Agency's internal Framework Document published in 1991. The purpose of the Framework Document is to set out clearly the customer–contractor relationship, with the Minister contracting with the

Agency to deliver particular services. The Chief Executive is given a specific and, where possible, specified set of objectives together with specified overall resources. By means of the Framework Document, and the attendant strategic and business planning process which follow from it, the Chief Executive's responsibilities and accountability for the delivery of services are determined. The respective roles of the Minister, the Permanent Secretary of the Department of Health and Social Services and the Chief Executive of the SSA are illustrated in Appendix 1.3.

Agency Objectives

The SSA's overall objective, goals and key principles as reflected in its first strategic and business plan are set out in the box on page 10. The vision outlined reflects the important fact that the SSA serves multiple objectives, has a diversity of stakeholders and exists within a complex and uncertain environment.

That potential tensions might exist in delivering the visionary element of the strategic and business plan is well recognized by the Chief Executive:

> The Plan is the result of hard bargaining between those who allocate the resources and us, the providers of the services. And, of course, there will be a debate each year as to whether the resources are adequate to deal with the level of demand and the standards set. In the end it is for Government to decide what level of service it is prepared to fund and for the Agency to get the best possible value it can from those funds.

Contracts – The Framework Document

One of the key directives of the *Next Steps Initiative* is that chief executives are directly accountable to a minister in a quasi-contractual relationship and the foundation on which all executive agencies are built is therefore the Framework Document. Together with the strategic and business planning process, the Framework Document is designed to ensure that the responsibilities of the Chief Executive and the Minister are clearly defined.

As more and more agencies develop it is recognized that a number of conflicting interests need to be reconciled in a Framework Document. However, there lies in every Framework Document a paradox: how to give the

Components of the Agency's Vision

Our overall objective

Our overall objective is to meet the targets set by the Minister within the resources allocated and to do so efficiently, effectively and economically and with full regard for the varying needs and circumstances of its actual and potential customers, its staff and the interests of the taxpayer.

Our goals

To achieve our overall objective we have set the following goals for achievement over the next five years:

- The Agency will have established a reputation for efficiency and quality of service.
- Information and advice about benefits and services will be easily accessible to the public who will receive a speedy and accurate response to their enquiries.
- The Agency will continue to promote the take-up of benefits.
- Agency offices will be pleasant places for customers to visit and staff to work in.
- Managers will be organizing and delivering services in the way which best suits local community needs and will be held accountable for the results.
- Staff will have improved support through the increased use of information technology; they will be proficient, committed and proud to work in the Agency.
- Authority and responsibility will have been devolved to the optimum level.
- The Agency will provide an efficient service to Ministers in implementing legislative changes and providing information and advice on operational issues.
- The Agency will be providing an efficient and effective service to those Departments and Agencies with whom it has contracts.

Our key principles

We believe our goals will best be achieved by the adoption of a number of key principles. The four key principles which will under-pin all Agency activity are: good quality services, efficient services, proficient and valued staff and delegated personal responsibility.

Source: Social Security Agency (NI), *The Business Plan*, 1991–92, London: HMSO.

Chief Executive the necessary flexibilities to run the business of an agency yet maintain accountability to the Department. The nature of this paradox found in the accountability interrelationships specified in a Framework Document is that:

- ministers, supported by their departments, must set clear policy objectives and robust performance targets and monitoring arrangements for their agencies;
- Treasury must retain a central responsibility for trends in public service costs and maintain the containing of expenditure as a key objective; and
- chief executives are entitled to expect that they will have power to act in accordance with their judgement without unwarranted interference.

Resolving the inherent paradox within framework documents can best be achieved, according to the Efficiency Unit, by developing and maintaining a clear and shared vision of what the Agency is there to do through the establishment of agreed roles and objectives for all parties. In particular, this involves clarifying responsibility for specifying service standards and for monitoring their achievement. The Efficiency Unit's view is that 'It is the identification of the right targets and confidence in the systems which underpin them which are at the heart of a healthy arm's length relationship between Departments and Agencies.' Thus the Efficiency Unit envisage that the Minister's role is essentially a strategic one and that there is little need for intervention in the matters of day-to-day management of an agency. It is for the Minister to determine the difficult question of what service standards, within resource constraints, are acceptable. This can be achieved by setting a handful of robust and high-level targets to measure financial performance, efficiency and quality of customer service. Departments can assist Ministers in this process and can also challenge the performance of the Chief Executive in meeting targets. Chief Executives, on the other hand, are responsible for addressing how these demands should be met and need to be given assistance in this process by the Department through the timely provision of any new policy initiatives and forecasted workloads.

Major Issues for the Agency

There is an in-built impetus created by agency status to engage in more rigorous strategic and business planning. A major difficulty for the Agency has been the mismatch of the strategic and business planning cycle and the Public Expenditure Survey PES cycle, although these have been reconciled and 1994 was the first year where both cycles were synchronized.

The environment within which the Agency operates is increasingly turbulent and numerous threats confront it. For instance, it is anticipated that there will be continued constraints on public expenditure and tight budget management. The continued introduction of new policies and schemes at short notice, plus the Agency's overriding legal obligation to process all claims, can be expected to create pressures on the Agency. Similarly, the increased introduction of market testing (where an agency's activities are scrutinized to consider whether the private sector could do the job better) poses particular problems for the Agency given that it is not entirely geared to withstand competition.

If the SSA's core business is defined as 'money transmission' there are interesting dimensions to what could lie in the future, especially in light of such technological developments as smart cards and electronic funds transfer schemes. Thinking in these terms invites the Agency to use banks and building societies as the evaluation basis for the comparative cost efficiency of service delivery.

Efficiency is a key strategic issue for the SSA and achieving 'more with less' is a touchstone within all the Agency's policies. Every aspect of service delivery is therefore kept under constant scrutiny. This pursuit of cost efficiency could mean future staff reductions; the move to 'one-stop shops' with a consequent rationalization of the network of benefit offices; the application of business process redesign to streamline administrative procedures and processes; more intensive use of information technology and further moves towards a more rigorous cost management financial regime.

Measuring Performance

The SSA's service targets are set out in Appendix 1.4. Senior managers in the SSA believe that the current arrangements for setting targets might be improved. The approach taken by the DHSS in deciding what service standards should be applied in the SSA is simply to mirror, where appropriate, the targets set for the Benefits Agency. While these targets are extensive, the appropriateness of many of them is the subject of much debate within the Agency. This debate revolves around the balance to be struck between quality of service, financial and efficiency targets. In the words of the Chief Executive, 'there is a need to put much more emphasis on measuring quality'. Operational managers and staff in the SSA share this concern, particularly where meeting the targets set by the Minister means that 'staff can often only achieve the current clearance times targets set at the expense of the quality of service'.

Performance measurement is central to the ethos of an agency. According to one senior manager: 'Performance indicators are not value-free technical instruments of measurement. Rather, they reflect the various interest positions of different stakeholders, where each has a legitimate concern for meaningful information about the Agency's performance.' What performance criteria are used, who sets these and whose interests are being served by the evaluation of performance are therefore important issues for management accountability by the Agency to various stakeholders. To date, the stakeholder having least impact on the development of performance indicators is the client/customer. This is not to deny that 'customer service' is an important concern within the Agency. In keeping with other public service organizations, and influenced by the Citizen's Charter, the Agency has spawned its own variant of the ubiquitous 'customer charter'.

The performance indicators for the Agency, given that they basically replicate those for the Benefits Agency, provide a benchmark with the performance of this sister organization.

Workload Forecasting

Related to the issue of targets is the question of workload forecasting. Forecasting is a critical activity for any service organization as it determines resource requirements based on projected demand. This is a particularly important issue when it comes to social security provision where accurate predictions of the future demand for benefits can be difficult. Unlike Trading Fund Agencies, which have a measure of control over their own demand forecasting, the SSA is entirely dependent on another party, namely the Department of Health and Social Services. Such an arrangement creates in-built tensions, especially when demand projections prove to be incorrect, as happened, for instance, with the introduction of the new benefits for the disabled in 1992. The end result of this inaccuracy was that the initial resources allocated to implement these new benefits were insufficient and the mechanism for allocating additional resources to handle excess demand proved unsatisfactory. As one senior manager within the Agency reveals, 'Whilst there is an explicit approach to the handling of unforseen change reflected in the Agency's Framework Document, to either provide for additional resources in such circumstances, or, if not, to have the flexibility of adjusting existing targets or priorities, the reality is that this has not happened fully in practice'.

Management Accountabilities

The issue of accountability is at the centre of much debate surrounding agencies. A major reason for establishing agencies was to achieve more accountable management by placing responsibility and accountability for all operational matters under the control of a chief executive. This involves a change in accountability arrangements, where Permanent Secretaries, in their capacity as accounting officers, are no longer solely responsible to Parliament for all policy and operational matters relating to an agency. The extent to which accountability is 'shared' with an agency chief executive is both an important and sensitive issue. (See Appendix 1.5 for details of financial flexibility.)

Many of the issues surrounding accountability appear, prima facie, to have been resolved with the establishment of chief executives as accounting officers who are now liable to answer to the Public Accounts Committee on the responsibilities allocated to them in the Framework Document. This, theoretically, leaves the Permanent Secretary, as Departmental Accounting Officer, liable to answer for matters in the Framework Document specially assigned to the Department, rather than the Agency.

The Efficiency Unit recently highlighted the need for on-going development of the accountability issue. It is recognized, for instance, that the current text of the Accounting Officer Memorandum needs to be reviewed. By reason of the implications that can be drawn from the current wording, wide responsibility is ascribed to the Permanent Secretary for ensuring good management and financial propriety throughout the Department, *including agencies*. According to the Efficiency Unit, interpretation of this wide responsibility can mean that 'Certain sponsor Departments feel that they have to carry out their control and monitoring role in a closer and more detailed manner than might otherwise be the case, so as to provide the Permanent Secretary with a reasonable level of assurance, not just on the adequacy of control systems, but also on the activities of the Agency.'

The scope of the Permanent Secretary's wide responsibility is reflected in the Social Security Agency Framework Document, paragraph 4.7: 'As Agency Accounting Officer, the Chief Executive can be summoned to appear before the Public Accounts Committee (PAC). Where the Committee is examining Agency matters, it may require both the Permanent Secretary and the Chief Executive to appear before it.' This relationship has been put to the test recently when the Chief Executive of the SSA was called before the Public Accounts Committee (PAC) on a wholly operational matter. The Chief Executive attended the PAC alone and the Department did not intervene. However, in the words of the Chief Executive: 'There still exists within the Accounting Officer relationship an indeterminate shade of grey where "the hands off – hands on" dilemma has yet to be determined.'

Devolving responsibility down the line, not only from departments to agencies, but also within agencies from senior levels of management to those at more junior levels, is a major issue. This mirrors the belief implicit in the *Next Steps Initiative* recommendation that real change is much more likely to happen if individuals are held personally responsible for action and results.

From its inception the SSA has recognized the importance of creating new forms of management accountability through its key principle of 'delegated personal responsibility'. Devolution of responsibility for budgets, estate management and personnel management functions have been instigated. Equally, the development of a new management style which encourages individuals at all levels to take responsibility for dealing with problems and making improvements is strongly supported by top management in the Agency. There are limits though to which this aspect of the Agency's vision might be pursued. As one senior manager puts it:

The hard fact of life is that what is possible in terms of more enriched, responsible jobs for some of the lower levels of staff within the agency hits a bit of a brick wall when applied to the highly repetitive, specialised clerical work that people are engaged in. Of course, it is not impossible to change this, but it requires a root and branch revision of our business processes and also our culture.

Changing Personnel Practice

The Agency is committed to moving away from the traditional concept of management within the civil service as being about a process of management control and supervision. The Chief Executive of the SSA affirms the importance of the need for a more enlightened approach to management practice within the new agency framework:

> Our management and our staff resources are our greatest asset and it will be their commitment, their energy and their proficiency which will provide the spark of vitality needed for the Agency to succeed. Our objective is enlightened management policies, which take account of the expectations of our staff and the needs of a business and customer culture.

The way forward for the Agency is seen to require a major change in management style to bring about greater delegation, acceptance of responsibility and accountability, and greater scope for staff using initiative. The ideal state hoped for is that the Agency will move from 'management by command, driven by a system to be observed' to a new state of 'management by contract, driven by commitment to the job to be done'.

It is against this background that the SSA set about taking full advantage of its status to use whatever personnel flexibilities it could get towards achieving the desired cultural change. Appendix 1.6 outlines the flexibilities which the Agency enjoys in relation to the personnel regime, in relation to pay and grading, recruitment, performance appraisal and career development and training. It is in using the scope for personnel flexibilities that the SSA has sought to make progress in adopting a distinctive 'agency' approach to differentiate it from the personnel regime existing within the Northern Ireland Civil Service.

During its first operational year the Agency undertook a major review of its personnel strategies. The stated aim in its first business plan was 'to develop a personnel management strategy which is best suited to the needs of the Agency and makes best use of the personnel flexibilities delegated to the Agency in the Framework Document'. This strategy is focused on a move away from traditional personnel practice and aims to embrace the concept of human resource management. The key themes that underpin this strategy are:

1 Empowering line managers
   • devolution of personnel functions;
   • computer support;
   • discipline and inefficiency.
2 Performance appraisal
   • appraisal;
   • performance-related pay;
   • grading.
3 Proficient and valued staff
   • training and management development;
   • staff welfare;
   • induction;
   • staff benefits and incentives;
   • working patterns.
4 Right people in the right place at the right time
   • recruitment;
   • postings;
   • succession planning;
   • promotion;
   • manpower planning.

By setting a number of corporate objectives around the Agency's key principles of Proficient and Valued Staff and Delegated Personal Responsibility (see Appendix 1.7), additional commitment is provided for a new HRM regime.

Immediate attention was given by the SSA to the deficiencies that existed in the NICS appraisal scheme inherited by the new Agency. The existing appraisal system was found to have a number of serious deficiencies:

• Over 70 per cent of staff are assessed as very good or better, which creates difficulties in setting higher standards and results in the silting up of the performance pay arrangements.

- There is insufficient rigour in the assessment of performance so that assessments have become inconsistent, bland and meaningless.
- Many of the aspects of performance which are assessed are unsuitable or irrelevant to the new values and culture of the Agency.
- Many forward job plans are poor and staff do not receive sufficient feedback on performance on a regular basis.
- Unnecessary time, effort and expectation is involved in annual promotion assessments.

A Human Resource Strategy for the Social Security Agency (NI), 1992 (internal document)

By 1993 the SSA was successful in introducing a new appraisal system which had a number of attractive features for staff. In particular, it provides open and optional promotion assessments, joint appraisal and regular reviews of performance and makes use of a competence framework to identify development needs. Introducing assessment based on outputs rather than inputs proved more problematical, however, as there was an inability to set consistent and meaningful standards at the individual level and to measure these objectively, especially for the qualitative aspects of performance. In the words of one senior manager:

> The new system failed in this respect not because of the concept of measurable output objectives but because of the overlapping roles/tasks between grades, especially at middle management level, which make performance standards difficult to determine and promotability difficult to assess, and because of the attitudes and culture within the Agency which give appraisal and other associated managerial skills a low profile.

A review of the SSA's personnel strategy also reveals that there was a strong feeling among staff that the current system of performance-related pay is not achieving its objectives, with only 20 per cent of staff feeling that the system has a positive effect. While acknowledging the need to conduct an overall strategic review of the SSA's grading structure which focuses on the Agency's business needs and the need to be more efficient, the Agency Management Board recognizes that there is a need to proceed cautiously in this area. This is because:

The outcome of central pay negotiations is uncertain and the future direction volatile which does not allow for a sound planning foundation at present; there is a lack of empirical evidence on which to base decisions and a major pay and/or grading review could be potentially very disruptive at a time when substantial change is already underway.

From 1 April 1994, in line with government policy for Next Steps agencies, the SSA assumes responsibility for its own pay arrangements. In order to take full advantage of delegated pay arrangements it is envisaged that a full review of the existing pay and grading arrangements will be undertaken. Equal pay legislation is seen as a major limiting factor in devising new arrangements, as is the status of agency staff as employees of the DHSS. The net result, in the short term, of gaining delegated pay bargaining is described by one senior manager:

> Whilst delegated pay bargaining provides a platform to carry out a review of grading arrangements, there are limitations to the extent to which we can vary from the central settlement under the present grading arrangements. The other real issue to be addressed is the 'rules of engagement' for establishing future negotiations with Agency Trade Union Side – the latter will want a commitment to parity with the rest of the NICS, whilst the SSA will want flexibility to establish grading which best suits their needs and which they can afford.

Empowering Line Managers

Establishing clearer and more accountable management responsibility means that the SSA is committed, under its key principle of Delegated Personal Responsibility, to devolve responsibility and authority for the provision of services to the lowest appropriate level. In its Annual Reports the Agency has shown successful examples of delegating responsibility downward in the organization. For instance, managers locally are now responsible for a range of issues, from training through to manpower budgets, discipline, absentee management and inefficiency. However, not everyone in the Agency agrees that the existing process of devolution has led to radical results. One view is that the Agency is only tinkering with systems. In the words of one line manager:

Local managers need the power to pull the levers that count in delivering a front line service. Operating under the existing terms and conditions of the NICS limits the flexibility of local managers as they have to work within the existing transfer and mobility restrictions. This can result in them having to manage with a surplus in one grade and an under supply in another. In particular, they need to have the right to 'hire and fire' if they are to create a more overtly based performance culture.

The most notable commitment from the SSA Management Board in carrying forward changes needed to improve performance and efficiency lies in the area of management training and development. A new training and development strategy has been developed which, in the view of the Personnel Director:

> . . . focuses on matching the business needs and new cultural change needed in the Agency through the introduction of competency based training. This approach requires renewed emphasis on roles and responsibilities to ensure that everyone in the Agency knows what is expected of them and has the opportunity to acquire the skills and knowledge needed to perform their jobs and to fulfil their full potential.

The Agency believes that to match training against 'what staff need to be good at doing in order to meet business needs more effectively' requires a competence approach within training and management development. A bespoke competence framework has been developed by the SSA which clearly sets out the skills, knowledge and experience required for effective performance in any given grade. This competence framework is also being used in the further evolution of the staff appraisal system.

Management training in the Agency is ring-fenced since Agency Board members believe that commitment to training gives tangible expression to the Agency's key principle of 'proficient and valued staff'. The Chief Executive regularly affirms the Agency's commitment to training and management development:

> We will only be able to meet the challenges facing the Agency through a well trained and motivated workforce. We recognise that managers of to-morrow will no longer be people who have mastered one discipline as the passport to a lifetime's career. More than ever, we require our managers to be learning continually, updating old skills and acquiring new ones. They need to be flexible and innovative, to be visionaries and leaders and to be coaches and

developers of staff much more than the controllers of the past. We are therefore committed to training and development and to providing managers with
the necessary skills to meet the challenges and opportunities facing them.

Staff Attitudes

Through the mechanism of a staff attitude survey, the Agency Board
attempts to gauge staff response to the ongoing process of change within
the Agency. The following are the key findings of a staff attitude survey
conducted during 1992:

- 89 per cent of staff are committed to improving the quality of service
  they deliver
- 44 per cent of staff say the quality and efficiency of the service has
  improved since the Agency was established
- 21 per cent of staff feel that most customers have a high opinion of the
  service delivered by the Agency
- 75 per cent of staff say they have a good understanding of their Branch's
  aims and objectives
- 49 per cent of staff are satisfied with their present job
- 13 per cent of staff feel that the Agency cares strongly for its staff
- 58 per cent indicated that they would leave the Agency if offered a
  comparable job in the wider Civil Service
- 89 per cent are clear about the standard of performance expected of
  them in their current job
- 58 per cent of staff do not regard the promotion process as fair to all
  staff
- 50 per cent of staff said that initiative and innovation were rarely praised
- 33 per cent of staff believe that the findings of the survey will be put to
  good use

(*Source*: Staff Attitude Survey, Social Security Agency (NI), 1992 (internal
document))

The Future

In April 1994 the Department of Finance and Personnel announced that
there were to be job losses within the NICS involving some 2,300 staff.

The pressure for cost efficiency continues to be a major fact of life facing all government departments in Northern Ireland.

Writing in the preface to the Agency's 1993–97 strategic plan, the Chief Executive highlighted the difficulties that lie ahead in turning the Agency's vision into reality:

> The incoming year is likely to be the most difficult we have had so far. It will require all of us to give our best and to tackle the tasks we face with deter- mination and vigour. Although perhaps slower than we would wish, I am confident that we can still make further good progress in turning the Agency's vision into reality.

In August 1994 the Agency announced the details of a scheme for voluntary redundancies among staff.

Discussion Questions

1 How can agencies resolve the paradox inherent in the relationship between the agency and its parent department?

2 Are the performance measures adopted by the agency appropriate for measuring the agency's efficiency and effectiveness?

3 How compatible are the core values of 'delegated personal re- sponsibility' and 'proficient and valued staff' with the realities of Social Security Agency life?

4 Does the agency meet the needs and demands of all its stakeholders?

Appendix 1.1: The Vision for Agencies

Traditionally, the way the Civil Service is organized makes it difficult to achieve a proper balance between policy and delivery. This, argued the authors of the *Next Steps Initiative* report, has led to managerial weak- nesses in government, with an emphasis, for instance, on the role of civil servants servicing ministers rather than managing their departments. The complexity and diversity of work in many departments, plus an imposed bureaucratic method of working, serves to constrain the freedom of civil servants to adopt a much-needed new approach towards the delivery of public services. Next Steps agencies, according to advocates of reform, create a more liberating approach to the business of government where civil servants have greater freedom to 'manage' rather than simply to 'administrate'.

The *Next Steps Initiative* recommended that agencies should be established to carry out the executive functions of government, as distinct from policy advice, and be headed by a chief executive. Agencies operate within a Framework Document which should clearly set out objectives and targets. Agencies should also enjoy a set of new financial and personnel freedoms if they are to achieve the required (better) performance.

It is recognized in the *Next Steps Initiative* report that structure alone cannot achieve the benefits to be gained from an increased business focus in the delivery of government services. To maximize results, and release the necessary managerial energy for the task, central constraints on managers ought to be loosened and a more overtly performance-based culture created.

Achieving the vision of agencies requires profound organizational change and this is neatly summarized in the *Next Steps Initiative* report as:

- greater clarification of roles and responsibilities to develop a clear sense of identity, purpose and direction and to establish clearer and more accountable management responsibility;
- contracts, clarifying the expected outputs and aggregate inputs and focusing greater attention on their achievement through greater precision about the results expected of people;
- greater incentives to good performance;
- greater management flexibility, putting the stress on results rather than processes; and
- strengthened commitment from the top, to carry forward the changes needed to improve performance and efficiency.

It is against this background that over 96 Executive Agencies have been established. There are various species of agency which differ in the range of activities they are concerned with and which have varied forms of financial regime. Some agencies are more clearly differentiated in their 'executive' role while others remain less clearly separated from their involvement in policy making.

Appendix 1.2: Agency Management Board

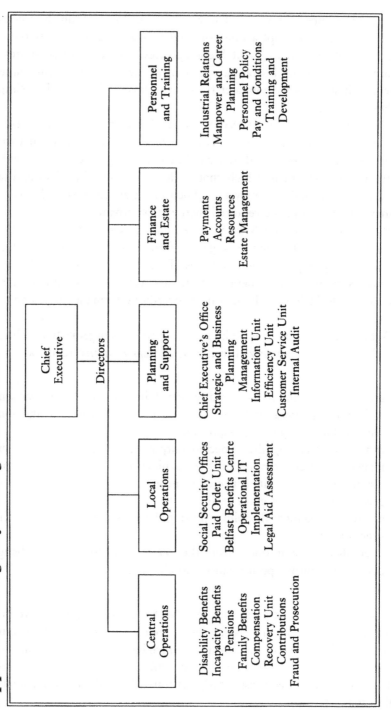

Chief Executive

Directors

Central Operations
- Disability Benefits
- Incapacity Benefits
- Pensions
- Family Benefits
- Compensation Recovery Unit
- Contributions
- Fraud and Prosecution

Local Operations
- Social Security Offices
- Paid Order Unit
- Belfast Benefits Centre
- Operational IT Implementation
- Legal Aid Assessment

Planning and Support
- Chief Executive's Office
- Strategic and Business Planning
- Management Information Unit
- Efficiency Unit
- Customer Service Unit
- Internal Audit

Finance and Estate
- Payments
- Accounts
- Resources
- Estate Management

Personnel and Training
- Industrial Relations
- Manpower and Career Planning
- Personnel Policy
- Pay and Conditions
- Training and Development

Figure 1.1 *Agency Management Board*

Appendix 1.3: Roles and Responsibilities

1   The Minister defines the scope of the Agency's activities; agrees its Strategic and annual Business Plans and sets its annual performance targets and resources.

2   The Permanent Secretary, as Permanent Head of the Department and principal adviser to the Minister, is responsible for those matters affecting the management of the department as a whole and for ensuring that adequate systems are in place across the department to support this role. The Permanent Secretary is also responsible for advising the Minister about the policy, resources plans, objectives, targets and performance of the Agency and for monitoring, on the Minister's behalf, the performance of the Agency and the Chief Executive.

3   The Chief Executive is responsible for the effective operation of the Agency in accordance with this document, his letters of appointment, and the Agency's agreed Strategic and annual Business Plans, and for meeting its objectives and targets within the resources allocated. In addition, it is his responsibility to:

•   obtain the Minister's approval to changes in the Strategic and Business Plans which the Chief Executive considers necessary;
•   alert the Minister and the Department to any aspect of the Department's activity which affects significantly the Agency's ability to perform effectively;
•   provide the Permanent Secretary with the information required for monitoring, on behalf of the Minister, the Agency's performance against its specified targets and for policy development and related purposes, including the forecasting of benefit expenditure; and
•   ensure that responsibility and management authority within the Agency is extensively devolved and keep all aspects of the management and organization of the Agency under review to ensure they best suit its business needs.

Appendix 1.4: Performance Indicators

Table 1.1 Service targets and performance

Area of work	Targets 1992–93	Achieved 1992–93	Targets 1993–94
Social Fund			
Crisis loans	application cleared day need arises	same day	same day
Community Care grants	7 days	6.23 days	65% in 7 days 95% in 20 days
Income Support			
Claims	4 days	3.35 days	71% in 5 days 90% in 13 days
Accuracy	99%	99%	92%
Sickness – Invalidity Benefit			
Claims	65% in 12 days 95% in 30 days	68.84% in 12 days 89.08% in 30 days	65% in 10 days 95% in 30 days
Accuracy	98%	98%	97%
Child Benefit			
Claims	65% in 10 days 95% in 30 days	73.19% in 10 days 93.33% in 30 days	73% in 10 days 95% in 30 days
Family Credit			
Claims	60% in 13 days 95% in 45 days	61.15% in 13 days 98.03% in 45 days	60% in 13 days 95% in 42 days
Accuracy	96%	98.49%	92%
Disability Living Allowance			
Claims	60% in 30 days 95% in 55 days	35.45% in 30 days 52.29% in 55 days	65% in 30 days 85% in 55 days
Accuracy	96%	98.03%	96%
Disability Working Allowance			
Claims	95% in 5 days	68.49% in 5 days	
Accuracy	95%	98.45%	
Pensions			
Claims	65% in 20 days 95% in 60 days	74.23% in 20 days 94.37% in 60 days	65% in 20 days 95% in 60 days
Accuracy	99%	99.71%	99%

Table 1.1   Cont'd

Area of work	Targets 1992–93	Achieved 1992–93	Targets 1993–94
Unemployment Benefit			
Claims	8 days	7.62 days	7.5 days
Customer satisfaction			
% satisfied customers	90%	86%	90%

Source: Social Security Agency (NI), Annual Report and Accounts 1992–1993, HMSO, London.

Table 1.2   Efficiency and performance

Area of work	Target 1992–93	Achieved 1992–93
Social Fund		
Social Fund loan recovery	£13.62m of loan expenditure to be covered by loan recoveries	£15.07m of loan expenditure covered by loan recoveries
Live within gross allocation for loans and grants	£26.33m	£26.30m
Income Support		
Recovery of Income Support overpayments	£1.0m	£0.93m
Fraud		
Gross annual benefit saving	£10.40m	£10.56m
Contributions		
Increase the number of surveys to	5,000	7,987

Source: Social Security Agency Annual Report and Accounts 1992–1993, London: HMSO.

Appendix 1.5: Financial Flexibilities

Subject to normal supply procedures, and the Permanent Secretary's approval of the Agency's financial management systems, the Chief Executive has authority to:

1 authorize capital projects within such limits as will be specified from time to time by the Permanent Secretary;
2 deploy the Agency's overall running costs allocation flexibly, except that services undertaken for the Benefits Agency for the Department of Social Security are covered by a separate running costs budget;
3 carry forward underspends of running costs and capital within limits specified by the Permanent Secretary and with the agreement of the Permanent Secretary;
4 vire from running costs into capital or other non running-cost subheads within the same section up to a maximum of 5 per cent of the donor subhead and 10 per cent of the recipient subhead (whichever is the lesser) in any financial year subject to the approval of the Permanent Secretary. The ceiling will apply to the total involvement from or to any subhead over the financial year;
5 change provision within subheads where the change is below 10 per cent of the relevant entry provisions in any financial year, provided that the amount does not exceed 10 per cent of the recipient line entry;
6 reinvest each year in its business a proportion of efficiency savings, the proportion to be agreed with the Minister and, where appropriate, the Department of Finance and Personnel.

Appendix 1.6: Personnel Flexibilities

Pay and Grading

1 The Agency's pay and grading structure is consistent with Northern Ireland Civil Service standards.
2 The Agency will, in consultation with the Department and the Department of Finance and Personnel, review its pay and grading structure to ensure that it meets its business needs.
3 Subject to the agreement of the Department and the Department of Finance and Personnel, the Agency may establish an efficiency-related bonus scheme for staff.

Recruitment

1 The Agency has authority to recruit permanent staff below Executive Officer Grade II directly through the Civil Service Commission.
2 Recruitment of permanent staff at Executive Officer Grade II and above is in agreement with the Permanent Secretary and through the Northern Ireland Civil Service Commission.
3 The Agency may bring forward proposals, for approval, by the Department and the Department of Finance and Personnel, for alternative methods of recruitment.
4 The Agency has authority to recruit directly staff, up to and including Grade 6, on short-service contract, or casual or limited appointment. All recruitment is by fair and open competition and on merit.

Staff Appraisal

1 The Agency operates the performance appraisal system in use in the rest of the Northern Ireland Service.
2 It may adapt the system to meet its own requirements following consultation with the Department and the Department of Finance and Personnel.

Career Development and Training

1 The Agency is responsible for promoting the training and development of all its staff.
2 In pursuit of this, it will develop a training and development strategy which meets the needs of the Agency and takes account as necessary of the broader needs of the Department.

Appendix 1.7: Extracts from the Social Security Agency's Strategic and Business Plans

Good-quality Services

1 improve the Agency's understanding of and responsiveness to customer requirements by introducing regular independent sampling of customer opinion on the quality of service;

2   invest in customer care training for agency staff and recognize the importance of quality through the introduction of Quality of Service Officers in all Management Units;
3   make the service more accessible by trialing new Customer Service Access Points to provide the full range of services in some areas at present not well served by current outlets.

Efficient Services

1   implement Operational Strategy Computer Systems to improve the services to the unemployed and the disabled;
2   set up service development teams to produce more efficient methods of working, taking account of the opportunities provided by Operational Strategy Computer Systems;
3   develop and improve the systems for financial and management accountability and control.

Proficient and Valued Staff

1   develop and implement a training and development strategy which is more appropriate to the changing needs of the Agency, with renewed emphasis on customer service training;
2   develop a personnel management strategy which is best suited to the needs of the Agency and which makes best use of the personnel flexibilities delegated to the Agency in the Framework Document;
3   develop and introduce revised and streamlined industrial relations arrangements which are focused more sharply on the business needs of the Agency and which encourage resolution of issues expeditiously and at the lowest level possible;
4   introduce regular sampling of staff opinion and satisfaction.

Delegated Personal Responsibility

1   devolve responsibility for personnel management to local management unit level;
2   devolve certain centrally held budgets to Management Units;
3   review roles and responsibilities of all grades within each Management Unit to ensure responsibility is delegated to the appropriate level;

4   encourage local and other initiatives by introducing a scheme to foster innovation.

References

CM 1760, *Improving Management in Government – the Next Steps Agencies Review 1991*, HMSO, London, November 1991.
CM 2101, *The Citizens Charter First Report: 1992*, HMSO, November 1992.
Social Security Agency (NI), 'A Human Resource Strategy for the Social Security Agency', 1992 (internal document).
Social Security Agency (NI), *Annual Report and Accounts, 1991–1992*, London: HMSO.
Social Security Agency (NI), *Report of Findings of Customer Survey*, 1992, HMSO, London.
Social Security Agency (NI), Staff Attitude Survey, 1992, (internal document).
Social Security Agency (NI), *The Business Plan*, 1991–92, London: HMSO.
Treasury and Civil Service Committee 7th Report, The Next Steps Initiative, (HC 496), London: HMSO, July 1991.

2

Strategic Change at Kirby College*

Julie Rayner

Change – social, economic and technological – has become a necessary part of life for most organizations. Change has its enemies, and the more fundamental the change the stronger the emotional response it is likely to bring about. Dealing with this response and implementing change successfully makes considerable demands on the managers involved. This case study examines the implications of corporate status for a further education college and the impact on the organization and its staff following the decision to remove post-16 colleges from local education authority (LEA) control. The Background Note (p. 51) supplies further details of the change.

Kirby College, Middlesbrough

In terms of full time equivalent students (FTEs) Kirby College is among the largest of the further education colleges in Cleveland. Although there are two other colleges of a similar size, it has the geographic advantage of being at the centre of the county. The population of Middlesbrough is approximately 141,089, falling from 141,962 in mid-year 1991. Approximately 6,402 students currently attend programmes at the college, although not all are from Middlesbrough, many travelling from the surrounding towns.

Other non-student visitors come to enjoy the training restaurant, the fast-food restaurant, the range of hair-styling and beauty treatments as well as plays and other public events. The college could be described as having

---

* This case draws upon interviews with lecturers and senior managers in Further Education Colleges in Cleveland.

a high profile in the community, having been established in 1966 and occupying a building part of which was originally a grammar school constructed in 1911. There are a number of specialist classrooms, a beauty salon, a hairdressing salon, a hotel reception, an access centre and a library, all being specifically designed to support the teaching and training which takes place.

The college has 130 full-time lecturers employed to deliver education and training. They are supported by approximately 74 members of ancillary staff (including part-time employees) made up of administrative staff, technicians and craft technicians. There are a further 150 visiting lecturers. The building is continually being enhanced and decorated. The college serves a variety of client groups which include 16–19 year olds, the local community, the hotel and catering industry, the business and banking professions and women returners wishing to update their skills. The college also offers clients a variety of modes of attendance, such as full-time or part-time study, or open learning (where the student works at his or her own pace in the college's access centre). Appendix 2.1 shows projected income and expenditure for 1994–5. The majority of income is from the central government through its funding council, the Further Education Funding Council (FEFC). There is potential for further income through full cost courses for local employers or through franchising arrangements.

At the moment the college could not physically accommodate more students as the existing buildings are at full capacity. Full-time staff are also fully committed within the current timetable requirements. It may be possible to build or rent new accommodation or employ more staff in growth areas. The college has extensive playing fields.

Structure

The principal of the college has a major role to play, not least that of the sole accounting officer with legal responsibilities. Under the new regime the college has developed a new management structure. Lecturers now have to take on management responsibilities for marketing, finance, estates and personnel. Responsibilities are devolved to senior lecturers who are currently in charge of divisions, and their job descriptions have altered accordingly.

The college was structured on traditional lines and was split into four faculties: Business Education, General Education, Hotel and Catering, and Tourism and Leisure. The head of faculty (HOF) was supported by heads of divisions (HODs). The college is looking to develop a matrix structure which will increase the management roles and lead to the appointment of four assistant principals. Senior academics are taking on more responsibilities in areas with which they are unfamiliar, for example in cost centre management. Faculty budgets are broken down into divisional budgets and those in turn are broken down into budget headings per programme. This requires a monitoring function for senior management. HODs are being given the responsibility for utilization of resources and involvement in such matters as capital bids, furniture and fittings. The HODs' roles were seen at all levels in the hierarchy as being very important. These are, after all, the people at the chalkface who manage the teams. It is predicted that heads of faculties will have to rely on them much more, because HOFs will be given other specialized responsibilities in functional areas of management such as personnel, estate management and finance. Teamwork and leadership ability were identified as the key factors to take the college successfully through incorporation.

Management implications

Although the college was generally thought by senior management to be very healthy in terms of attitudes and responsiveness towards incorporation, some members of staff expressed resistance to change which could have acted as a potential blockage to the successful adoption of incorporation: 'The senior lecturers themselves might decide that, if it's not dressed up in the right way . . . enough is enough.' Resistance could also have arisen from those senior lecturers who were happy with their existing functions: 'It's just a matter of inculturing (*sic*) people and creating change. I know I have to change my role, there is no point in getting excited about it.'

Despite the blockages identified, there appears to be confidence in the way incorporation was undertaken by the management team, but still concern as to whether members of staff possess the necessary skills following on from incorporation: 'We are getting there! We are taking consultants' advice, having meetings but whether we have the skills remains to be seen.'

The college is trying to anticipate the problems and their solutions and to create a structure and function which is sufficiently fluid to allow for yet greater change.

Managers expected a totally changed environment – without the safety-net of the LEA. The management team generally welcomed the change, but at lower positions, middle management and lecturers, the uncertainty was very apparent and was potentially disruptive.

There was a feeling in the college that there should be recruitment of some new specialist personnel or the contracting-in of services, as staff had no experience of, for example, payroll matters. However, it was considered appropriate to train staff from within the college to take on some of the new responsibilities in marketing, finance, estates and personnel. Doubt was expressed as to whether the necessary skills were available: 'Will four people, currently heads of faculty, match those four functional roles perfectly? Do they have the expertise, the background etc? – I don't know. Staff development will be required.'

In 1993–4 the college spent £65,000 on staff development. Fear was expressed that the 'Silver Book' which specifies terms and conditions for lecturers' contracts in further education would not be maintained in its current form in the future. Terms and conditions form part of the contract of employment, but these may be altered or varied by the employer. Lecturing staff in the new universities now have a reduced seven-week holiday, an example of a sector which has adjusted to its new environment. Market forces of the future may have the effect of driving up salaries for specialist teachers in areas of limited supply, and there was a suggestion from more than one source that staff may be headhunted in future. It was felt that unions would resist such differentiation in salaries as it could be seen as detrimental to the morale of their members. However, one manager stated:

> I have heard it said from industrialists, 'why do we have to pay hairdressers significantly more than they would earn in industry where they are demonstrating the same skills?' The argument is it is a different job – it is teaching. They seem to get into black and white arguments and I can see them saying in some colleges, 'if we are appointing someone in catering we will pay them less'. It is going to happen.

There is staff development funding available to colleges from the Government which is directed at management training. This could be directed towards middle management, such as section leaders, academic leaders and cross-college co-ordinators. This could prepare middle management for a future role which will make greater demands on them of a managerial nature. A number of colleges supported the view that incorporation would demand a great many more management skills from members of their organizations. It was clear that new responsibilities would be devolved to senior lecturers and they, particularly, would need staff development in managerial skills. It was also suggested in one case that the role of senior lecturers in the future would bring them on to the management spine and they should be rewarded them accordingly.

Within the salary scales set out in the 'Silver Book' is one which applies to members of staff carrying management responsibilities in addition to those of lecturing. It is known as the Management Spine and, in the 'Silver Book,' acknowledgement is made of the degree by which a member of staff's input into management should be rewarded financially. The greater the input the higher will be his or her position on the spinal column and the greater the financial reward. Appointments to the management spine shall be through negotiation with employers.

As one senior manager stated:

> We will obviously need to consider who should be going on general management courses in terms of developing management skills and experience because the whole structure of the college may need to change and more people need to be involved in the day to day management issues. Senior lecturers may have to have more management responsibility and come onto the management spine and be rewarded accordingly.

Culture

Managers recognized that changes would take place and require changes to traditional ways of working. Not only that but changes in attitudes, beliefs and values would be necessary. Senior managers expressed the following views:

> It will change, perhaps we have been protected in the public sector for a long time, we tend to work on the basis that our jobs are there 'til we don't want them anymore, but there is going to be more rapid change in terms of delivery, curriculum, context and people will have to get used to the idea that there will be a private sector inculturement (*sic*) driving the organization, not just at senior manager level, but right through the organization.

> The senior lecturer role will extend but programme co-ordinators and heads of faculties roles will be different as opposed to being extended.

Traditional academics may feel uncomfortable using such terms as 'marketing', 'selling', 'performance indicators' and 'profit' and may believe that they have no role to play in education.

Strategy

Prior to incorporation Kirby College appeared to have no clear-cut competitive strategy. Senior managers gave three different explanations of that strategy and another stated that the college did not have a competitive strategy as such:

> It is widely assumed that strategy is about choosing from a limited range of objectives. I mean that tends to be the industrial model, that there are some things you can't do, therefore you go for the ones you can do. Now I am not sure that is a very good model for the education service or a college like this because in an interventionist environment everybody seems to discover the meaning of life on an average of about once every six months – so you've got new objectives.

> Strategy is not about taking a narrow functional view. It is about taking an 'holistic' view of the situation and look at problems from a strategic perspective.

> Strategy making is of little relevance to organizational reality unless cultural aspects are explicitly understood.

> Set out your strategic objectives and work towards them but do remember that in a volatile business like ours which is essentially about human behaviour, about what people want to do – it's certainly not about the economic and determinist agendas which are set out by the Department of Employment in Westminster. This fall-back position which enables you to respond as the real world is and not what your prescriptive strategies are. . . . .

Organizations often seek to express their strategy in terms of a mission statement. Kirby College's mission statement was:

> To offer a service of high and measurable quality to all its students. The college will be a major provider of learning opportunities to all ages and ability ranges within the area. It is a centre of excellence for vocational, academic and personal achievement through programmes which enhance the employment opportunities, academic progression and personal and social growth of all its students, irrespective of gender, race or disability.

It is argued that the aims and objectives cannot be solely profit related. Indeed, by the very nature of a public body, it has to consider a wide span of concerns serving several masters, such as Central Government, the Funding Council, Teesside Training and Enterprise Council (TEC) and the local community. However, according to one senior manager: 'In terms of product, in terms of courses and students, the college will have to widen out into areas in which its not operating at the moment'. The expectations and objectives of different stakeholder groups are clearly important as they will affect acceptable strategies advanced by management. However, the beliefs and assumptions that make up the culture of an organization, although less explicit, will also have an important influence.

Another senior manager in Kirby College was convinced that the college competes on quality. That is, it is the best college, offering the best courses, and students get the best work placement and the best teaching experience. Evidence to support this quality ethos is seen in the employment of a principal lecturer in a quality development role and in the effort to achieve BS 5750 for the administrative procedures in the full cost course area of provision.

One manager claimed that, although the college as a whole does not have an explicit competitive strategy, other evidence suggested one particular faculty in the college certainly does have a competitive strategy. It may be the case that, left to its own devices, each functional department, or in the colleges terms, faculty, will inevitably pursue approaches dictated by its professional orientation and the incentives of those in charge.

There is a fear, in the further education world at large, of closure or merger if colleges are not seen by the Funding Council as being efficient and effective. One local vice-principal expressed the concern: 'I'm worried about competition because colleges in Cleveland are going to go to the wall; you have got to be realistic.' One possibility is merging with another college that has complementary areas of expertise, resources, courses or student profile.

Hitherto the LEA has provided a safety-net, and according to one senior officer from the LEA: 'In the past the LEA has been known to provide additional funds for colleges which have been over-budget but this is not going to happen in the future.'

Kirby College, however, views itself in a strong position as it has not been one of the over-spending under-utilized colleges in Cleveland. As one senior manager stated:

> I looked forward to incorporation because I saw it as an opportunity to get away from the LEA, and break free from a lot of the restrictions we have had. I feel Kirby has subsidized a lot of the other colleges – we have been

full, efficient, effective. Other colleges have overspent and been artificially inflated by manipulated figures.

The competitive strategy within the college was unclear at senior management level, so, naturally, it cannot be communicated effectively to other hierarchical levels, or, if ideas are being communicated, they reflect conflicting views. As one senior manager stated: 'Our success is due to luck, we keep doing the right things because we have got highly motivated people in the college.'

Currently the college chooses different approaches to meet different circumstances. For example, when quoting for full cost work, attention is directed towards keeping the costs low. This resembles the adoption of a cost leadership strategy. In other areas, the best training and the best work placement experience may be offered to the student and this would demonstrate a product differentiation strategy.

Achieving a low overall cost position often requires a high relative market share and, as Kirby College may be described as having a high market share only in certain areas, it does not therefore have this advantage across the board. It competes with a similarly sized college in close physical proximity. It would be possible to adopt a cost leadership strategy but this would be very difficult unless the Funding Council will allow one college, undercutting another, to obtain a better market share. Even then this would be a dangerous strategy for Kirby College and only one college could win.

Further, approximately 80 per cent of the college's costs is accounted for in salaries. As private trainers pay less than colleges, keeping costs low would be a more appropriate strategy for them than for Kirby College. For example, a college could undoubtedly be run more cost efficiently if it were to pull out of low demand areas, or areas of education and training which are expensive to deliver, in favour of lucrative full cost work. However, this is not generally possible as the Government's objectives for colleges contain parameters which would not enable this type of generic strategy to be adopted. For example, the 'College Development Plan and Annual Programmes 1991–94' states: 'Within the limits of the Cleveland LEA policy on resourcing the College is committed to offering, to a wide academic and age range, courses of high quality and leading, where appropriate, to national qualification routes and opportunities for employment and personal growth.' This requires differentiating the product or service offered by the college from those offered by other colleges and to create something which is perceived, by the customer, as being unique. Approaches to differentiation can take many forms, such as: design or brand image; technology; features;

customer service; dealer network or other dimensions. One senior college manager suggests the approach will be possible in the form of course design:

> The strategy is a differentiated range of combinations, patterns and progression for the student. The college aim to put the product together in different ways for the student. That's what's going to happen to our courses. There's going to be a commonality (*sic*) of levels and a commonality (*sic*) of core skills.

Differentiation provides insulation against competitive rivalry because of brand loyalty by customers resulting in a lower sensitivity to price. Likewise, in the case of Kirby College students, once they enrol on a programme, with the obvious caveat that the quality of their experience in the college is the best, they will stay and progress to other programmes. This in turn increases margins and provides entry barriers to any other new competitors wishing to enter the industry.

The differentiated image of the college from other colleges may be achieved and sustained in different ways, for example careful selection of courses on offer or the technical excellence of the equipment. In this latter case the college's specialist facilities such as model offices, hotel reception, restaurants, computer rooms and beauty salons are very attractive. The access centre, tutor arrangements and facilities, the general appearance of the college and the strong student relations also assist the College in a differentiation strategy. It will be important to understand which of these activities are actually valued by students, by employers and by the Funding Council and to plan the utilization of resources accordingly.

'The College's strategy is going to be to persuade the University to franchise to us a number of its programmes. We have already been fairly successful at that' (Senior Manager). This linkage with Teesside University will allow the college to offer Higher National Diploma programmes, thereby enabling students to enter the college at 16 and progress from a National Diploma on to a Higher National Diploma, graduating some four years later. As one manager put it:

> Obviously programmes which become natural follow-ons from programmes we are already doing, like the Higher National Diploma in Business Studies, which will effectively convert many of your students from a two-year programme to a four-year programme. That means we are establishing a much larger pattern of provision into our curriculum – five years, four years, three years instead of two. So that the whole of the marketing effort we put into

picking up students isn't simply dissipated in a student who is staying here really for a few months.

A further point which would support this linkage is the proximity of Kirby College to the university, both being located in Middlesbrough. It is much more convenient for a Teesside university student to travel to Kirby College than to travel to other colleges in, say, Hartlepool, Billingham or Redcar.

Stakeholders

One of the distinctive features of managing in the public services is said to be the number of individuals or organizations that have an interest in those services, i.e. there is a multiplicity of stakeholders. We would suspect them to have different views, different values and have different abilities to affect the decision-making process.

The National Association of Teachers in Further and Higher Education (NATFHE)

NATFHE considers that further and adult education plus sixth-form colleges form too large and diverse a sector, with too strong local roots, to be planned and funded effectively by a national body without an effective, sensitive intermediate level of support. Further, education is a service and not a marketplace, and must be subject to local democratic planning and accountability. This view is supported by the Association of Colleges in Further and Higher Education (ACFHE) who are particularly aware of the huge diversity of this sector. Member institutions range from very small mono-technics with a little over 200 students full time equivalent (FTE) to the largest mixed economy institutions with several thousand FTEs.

NATFHE is concerned to protect the interests of its members and to ensure that local pay bargaining does not diminish the terms and conditions of its members.

Central government

One of the expressed objectives is an increase in the numbers of students coming into the academic and vocational training marketplace, to the point in 1996 when the Government hopes all 16 and 17 year olds leaving education will receive training credit vouchers.

Government, through the Employment Department and the Department for Education, is keen to promote:

- achievement of national targets and standards;
- increased efficiency;
- higher levels of participation;
- performance, monitoring and quality;
- responsiveness to labour markets and employers;
- the use of private finance to support capital programmes;
- flexible contracts of employment for staff.

The Local Education Authority

The major effects on education departments over the last few years have been brought about by the Education Reform Act (1988) (ERA). Local authorities have responded to that legislation by restructuring their departments and, when legislation is eventually phased in completely, many of the services currently offered by the local authorities will no longer be provided. It will be up to the academic institutions to decide if and how much of those services they are going to buy in from the LEA and elsewhere. For example, should they buy a local inspection service or staff development programme from the LEA since, in the future, these services may be available from other institutions?

Another important piece of legislation has affected services such as ground maintenance, caretaking, cleaning services and catering. It is the Local Government Act 1988 which introduced compulsory competitive tendering. There is no guarantee that local authorities will win contracts, and the implication is that if the contracts are not won it will be necessary for the LEA to shed staff and to reorganize their services on a more financially competitive basis.

These major pieces of legislation have had significant effects on local authorities. New structures have been formed and posts lost even before the new Act to incorporate colleges of further education had been introduced.

From an LEA point of view:

> Whatever we may call each other at least there is a local authority interested in working together with the colleges to serve the needs of their immediate community. All that, presumably, will be lost in the sense that jobs will disappear and will have to be replaced with something but we are not going to be replaced by people who have been working in the locality for any length of time, or even with background or experience with FE.

Whatever the political pressures, a senior officer stated that the LEA still intends to show an interest in marketing to colleges the local authority department's services such as architectural, secretarial, estates management and fiscal. Indeed, a general package of expertise could be established and it is perceived that this would be more attractive to the managers of the sixth-form colleges than to colleges of further education. The latter have had the benefit for some time of running their own delegated budgets and have a more clearly defined perception of the freedom available under incorporation.

An important consideration for the LEA is the extent to which colleges: 'take education beyond the college boundaries and into the community'. The LEAs' loss of further education responsibilities will leave them with residual duties including responsibility for the youth service, discretionary awards and education allowances. Responsibility for transport will also remain, with legislation promised to ensure that authorities treat full-time students aged 16–18 no less favourably than sixth-form students in schools. The LEAs will be given the task of providing the new regional councils (of the FEFC) with information about the range of education and training available in each of the schools and advising on the work and performance of the further education colleges.

ERA meant a change in the working relationships between the LEA and colleges. One college had suggested that:

> Colleges were given more responsibility and the governing body more power, but not complete power, and so a tension was set up. It could be argued that tension was set up to make things change. We have been at loggerheads for a long period of time with officers and sometimes elected members. When you get the opportunity to break away from these people you tend to say 'yes'.

Where there has been conflict with the LEA in the past, this was an opportunity to move away from such conflict. It also provided colleges with more freedom to develop opportunities without the constraints imposed, such as the requirement to remain within franchise areas allocated by the LEA and the freedom to deal directly with TECs. However, that welcome was tempered by the view that there will arise, as a result of that change, substantial and numerous new problems and that the service from the LEA will be missed.

Independence from the LEA could produce greater efficiencies. A firm belief exists that a substantial amount of unnecessary bureaucracy had emanated from the LEA in the past. However, there may be a sense of security in having the authority's support whether on personnel, legal, financial or payroll matters. Worries which were identified appear to originate from the fact that colleges have little expertise in these areas. The responsibility for estates management caused concern, as the fear of falling foul of the Health and Safety Act 1974 is very real, particularly for some older colleges.

Fears were expressed that the TEC will become more involved in education and will effectively be substituted for the LEA representation. Representatives from Teesside TEC did not see themselves as substituting for the LEA in this way but acknowledged preparation for their increasing interaction with colleges.

One college in particular communicated very clear support of the LEA and felt that moving away from their control could lead to duplication of provision because of the degree of free market enterprise which is expected to be allowed:

> We are in a good LEA and we have a good relationship with them. At the moment there are certain contentious issues particularly for senior managers but that's neither here nor there. If we move out of that, one of the things that is difficult is the degree of free market enterprise which I think could lead to duplication of provision and the kind of lunacy that stands for planning – dog eat dog and I think that will be injurious to a lot of people, not least students – people will lose an awful lot, and that's tragic.

Clearly, there is some regret about abandoning a system which has been built up by local planning, over a great many years, with local knowledge and which is generally considered satisfactory. Detailed knowledge of an institution and a particular region and commitment to long-term provision were considered preferable to the short-term goals of some colleges.

Teesside Training and Enterprise Council (TEC)

Teesside TEC was formed in April 1990 and is a private limited company run by an external board of 15 directors, comprising two-thirds industrial representation and one-third from the county council and voluntary bodies within Cleveland. The Teesside TEC has approximately 110 members of staff and a budget from the Government of £30 million. Its aim is to work with all sections of the community to build a positive commitment to training and enterprise and to facilitate activities to improve the level and quantity available (Teesside TEC's Corporate Plan 1991–4). To do this they have joined in partnerships with educational bodies and local authorities. TEC controls £2.1 million of the further education budget and funds a further 5/6000 trainees through youth training schemes from the £30 million. The TEC's strategic framework is in place at national, sectoral and local levels. TEC's nationally will operate a new fund of £20 million to help colleges meet critical labour-market needs.

Teesside TEC claim to have analysed the needs of the local market to assist them in planning training projects, and clearly have an influencing role to play. Teesside TEC had an informal network of meetings and set up a quasi-strategic group which had representatives from all sections of education, including pre- and post-16 and further and higher education. Representatives from the Teesside TEC indicated an increased interaction between individual colleges and the TEC. To accommodate that potential activity the Teesside TEC is already recruiting a new member of staff at a senior level.

The changes may be summarized as a diminishing role for the LEAs in terms of control and influence of further education colleges. No longer will they be the go-between purchasing courses from colleges on behalf of the Teesside TEC. TECs may choose to deal directly with colleges on an individual basis, rewarding flexible and responsive colleges and discriminating against those who will work not with TEC and deliver according to a TEC's business plans. This could lead to yet further competition between colleges.

Further Education Funding Council

The Further Education Funding Council (FEFC) is the body that administers finance on behalf of the Government. It has nine regional councils. Funding is primarily based on student numbers. Appendix 2.2 gives an indication of this. According to the FEFC 70 per cent of colleges are financially sound, 24 per cent are in a vulnerable position and 6 per cent are in a weak financial position.

Increasingly, funding may be related to outputs where colleges are funded according to the level and number of qualifications that students achieve. However, as one college vice-principal expressed it: 'I worry that output-related funding will lead to deteriorating standards. I also believe that some colleges have turned a blind eye to low marks and weak performance in order to ensure maximum qualifications. This could verge on fraud and is certainly wrong.' The same may apply to franchise courses where the parent institution will wish to maintain quality.

The FEFC is keen to promote links between colleges and TECs and TECs are consulted on a college's strategic plan. The FEFC has also been given additional funding for work-related further education.

The Local Environment

Cleveland County has six colleges offering further education. These colleges are: Cleveland College of Art and Design, Middlesbrough (also having an annexe in Hartlepool), a specialist college concentrating on the delivery of art and design; Cleveland Technical College, Redcar; Hartlepool College of Further Education, Hartlepool; Kirby College of Further Education, Middlesbrough; Longlands College of Further Education, Middlesbrough; and Stockton and Billingham Technical College. The latter operates on a split site, in Stockton and Billingham. It is fair to say that the county is well served by so many colleges in what is considered nationally to be a small geographical area. Further, it is the opinion of many that Cleveland is over-provided with colleges. This results in the people of Cleveland not expecting to travel long distances to enjoy the benefit of college services, contrasting favourably with other areas in the country. (See Appendix 2.3 for a breakdown of courses offered by the colleges.)

Increased attention by college managers to strategic planning has highlighted questions that have long been of concern to managers: what is driving competition in this industry?; what actions are competitors likely to take, and what is the best way to respond?; how will the education industry evolve?; how can colleges be best positioned to compete in the long run?

Rivalry exists among organizations and in this case is represented by competition among educators and trainers existing in the marketplace which includes further education colleges, sixth-form colleges and private trainers. Potential entrants to the marketplace include new private trainers, schools and sixth-form colleges. Substitutes to college-based training and education include open-college provision, books, education and training programmes on television and radio. Colleges may be inclined to market aggressively to attract new students and to try to retain existing students for a longer period. The changing resource formula which allocates to colleges a sum per student enrolment has to take into consideration the responsibilities which colleges have to adopt and the services they will have to provide.

The effects of incorporation, together with the demographic decline in the number of 16–19 year olds, have resulted in strong competition between the further education colleges and sixth-form colleges. An increased rivalry for adult markets will arise as sixth-form colleges will no longer be restricted to the 16–19 age group market.

Already sixth-form colleges are moving into less traditional education and training areas to attract more students, an example being the development of BTEC Business Studies Diplomas. The potential threat of greater development of educational programmes on television and radio has been identified previously by colleges. The Open College competes with open learning within colleges and may also be described as a substitute for open learning, although it may be seen that colleges have the advantage over the Open College in that they generally enjoy closer proximity to clients and offer accessibility to a personal tutor.

The bargaining power of buyers will be enhanced by incorporation as they will be able to select education and training programmes from providers who will be competing more fiercely to retain their market share. A survey of Cleveland colleges has indicated that increased competition will provide buyers with more choice and will probably result in cheaper or higher-quality provision. Unfortunately the buyers may not be able to judge the quality of the products offered and may be persuaded by aggressive marketing and advertising techniques.

The buyers of education and training include the Funding Council, the LEA for non-vocational education, Teesside TEC, the general public, Teesside University for franchise arrangements and local business. This could be extended to encompass institutions in North Yorkshire and Durham County as some students may be prepared to travel such distances for a particular course. The buyers will find their bargaining power increased through the competition which incorporation will bring. However, new markets for further education are already opening up in franchise arrangements with higher education establishments delivering higher national qualifications such as higher national diplomas and certificates.

Incorporation will bring new freedoms for colleges but with them new responsibilities. The LEA's powers to direct training through its strategic planning, franchising arrangements and its purchasing power is transferred mostly to the new Funding Council. Where, in the past, the LEA would buy training on behalf of the TEC, it will now be likely that colleges will develop partnerships with the TEC without the LEA acting as the go-between. This may effectively transfer a great deal of buying power to the TEC.

It seems unlikely that new colleges will enter a marketplace where so many further education and sixth-form colleges already exist. There may be potential, however, for colleges outside Cleveland who see distance learning as an area to develop and compete with colleges in Cleveland. Further opportunities identified by these colleges may be to provide outreach courses to centres. Another potential would be for a college to compete in new areas of provision for that college, that is, outside the accepted franchise areas in Cleveland.

Schools may be potential new entrants into the marketplace as they may seek funding by expanding their activities. For example, BTEC first certificates are an area which schools are currently developing and this will bring them into direct competition with some further education colleges.

Colleges in this geographic area may be forced into much greater competition and, whereas education has previously been about sharing and establishing good practice around the country, this competition will now undermine trust, with future success depending on better preparedness and being more commercially proactive.

Incorporation was viewed as having the potential for causing problems for the management and staff of colleges, requiring review of strategic plans and objectives, and establishing the major accountabilities to be discharged. Examples include financial affairs and banking, payroll, VAT and taxation, the management of sites, and personnel matters, with all the associated legislation. Some were optimistic about their particular college's ability to cope with the demands of incorporation. One vice-principal expressed the view: 'the challenge in further education is to do with the management of change. This College has been good at change; it's had to'.

It was also predicted that there would be much more local pay bargaining in which NATFHE and other union bodies will be very much more embroiled. Further, it was thought that the results could lead to differentiation in pay north and south of the country, and lower payments to those who teach in the parts of industry which are known to have low pay standards. The hairdressing and catering industries were put forward as examples.

Such outcomes, if realized, may affect equal opportunities as, generally, the lower end of the salary scale tends to be dominated by women. Other views did not agree that college management and governors would be involved with such negotiations, as it was believed that Central Government will still retain the overall control of pay bargaining. However, the example of principals' salaries, where a form of local bargaining has taken place, indicates that governors of some institutions have been prepared to show rewards by increasing salaries. New universities have been known to offer directors a company car as part of the reward package.

British Standard (BS) 5750 was a standard most colleges were trying to achieve to apply to their commercial administrative procedures. One college was not addressing BS 5750 quite as enthusiastically as others because they did not see it as an all-embracing method of assuring quality in further education. Nevertheless, quality issues were viewed as critical for colleges on the basis of performance-related funding and the colleges' ability to measure their performance and monitor the quality of that performance.

Four of the further education colleges were considering opportunities to contract out some of the colleges' expertise and specialized ability to other organizations as a way of bringing additional funding to the college and involving students in work experience. It was the view of these colleges that contracting out their service would be a realistic proposition for colleges with, for example, an exceptionally good printing resource, to become involved in commercial printing. There may also be opportunities in design, painting, decorating or building maintenance for others with such skills, expertise and resources. Trade union concerns about involvement with such commercial contracts must be considered, but clearly such potential lends itself more readily to some colleges than others. For example, colleges which provide vocationally orientated programmes such as painting, decorating and building, or possess resources which could provide a professional printing service are more likely to be able to react commercially than colleges which are more academically focused. There is evidence that some colleges are already being enterprising in such ways, but those opportunities appear to be limited for the traditional sixth-form colleges. As one manager put it: 'We could use some language students to do some translation – that's an expertise we have, perhaps computer science and information technology, but it is not as obvious in a sixth-form college.'

Some colleges may be better equipped to cope with the demands of incorporation than others because of their size and the expertise already available in the college. Smaller colleges in particular tended to have more specialized skills and, therefore, acknowledged the need to buy-in expertise such as personnel, accounts, estate management and legal advice.

Colleges could consider the joint purchase of expertise and engaging in some form of consortium with others like minded. One college, however, rejected the idea on the basis that, in an arena of competition, it is more

likely that colleges would come into conflict with each other within such
arrangements.

Mergers were often thought to be more likely to affect sixth-form
colleges than colleges of further education. There was a suggestion, however, that it would be in the interest of sixth-form colleges to choose to
work closely with colleges of further education. One manager appeared
sympathetic to the staff of sixth-form colleges, but the general view expressed was that they are unlikely to survive *in specie*. In one specific geographic area of Cleveland, it was pointed out:

> We have an adult education centre, three sixth forms, and a college of
> further education. Now it doesn't make sense to pay all those different
> institutions, commit all that expenditure to operate in 1994, managing every-
> thing four times over. You could have the same buildings, same activities
> going on, but managed by one group of people.

The 1993 Act on incorporation ensured a reorganization of post-16 education by market forces and the view was that sixth-form colleges would
be the likely casualties. There was evidence that three institutions were
involved in informal discussions with others on the subject of mergers and
the expectation was that mergers would take place. All the smaller colleges
in Cleveland, including the sixth-form college, indicated that they felt
vulnerable, as success as an incorporated body had a dependency on size in
terms of FTEs. Two other colleges saw opportunities for merging and,
although discussions at this stage had only been internal, there was a strong
expectation that their colleges will merge with smaller institutions.

Colleges predict that the culture of colleges will have to change and that
it may be necessary to buy people in as they did not believe members of
staff could acquire the skills necessary to cope with the responsibilities
incorporation would thrust at them. They also suggested that they would
home grow (train) current staff members to assume responsibility for some
of the new functional areas as they did not feel there would be sufficient
funds to offer contracts to a whole range of professional specialists.

Discussion Questions

1   What strategy should Kirby College adopt to survive and prosper
    in the new world of further education?

2 What are the strengths, weaknesses, opportunities and threats that face Kirby College?

3 How can Kirby College satisfy the interests of all its stakeholders?

4 What are the difficulties in persuading professionals to develop management skills?

Background Note

The Education Reform Act 1988 (ERA) introduced major changes for further education colleges in England and Wales. While remaining under the control of Local Education Authorities (LEAs), these colleges were given delegated responsibilities for their governance and management. Most had reconstituted governing bodies by April 1990, exercising a wider range of responsibilities than previously for the overall development and management of their college and for its income and expenditure. For example, the governing body became responsible, through the college principal, for the precise pattern of provision and for the decision as to how best to spend the allocated budget. It is also responsible for seeing that the college is well run, efficient and effective. The major effect of ERA has been to alter the relationship between LEAs and colleges where the board of governors assume increased and delegated responsibilities.

The Secretary of State announced in Parliament in March 1991 that, in the light of the experience of granting the new universities and colleges full freedom to respond to the demands of students and the labour market, the further education colleges were to have the same treatment as the polytechnics, that is, freedom from local authority control, by April 1993. In 1992 Parliament passed the Further and Higher Education Act resulting in incorporation for Kirby College. Thus on 1 April 1993 some 500 further education colleges achieved corporate status and moved from under the control of the LEAs. The rationale for this change was that self-government would encourage colleges to be more efficient, effective, flexible and responsive. The environment will be more competitive. According to one local commentator: 'The ethos of incorporation is supposed to be competition or entrepreneuralism in favour of the regular, highly regulated situation which is considered to have been the case in Cleveland.'

Appendix 2.1: Kirby College – Projected Income and Expenditure Account 1994–1995

Income	£000
FEFC grants	4,921
Education contracts[a]	457
Tuition fees and charges	407
Other grant income[b]	150
Other operating income[c]	300
Investment income	41
Total income	6,276

Expenditure	£000
Staff costs[d]	4,523
Other operating costs	1,443
Total expenditure	5,966

Surplus	310

[a] From LEA, TEC and higher education franchising
[b] Including European social funds
[c] Primarily from catering
[d] Primarily for 163, out of a total of 229 full-time equivalent lecturing staff

Appendix 2.2: The Further Education Funding Council Circular 94/30 7 November 1994

Information from colleges in their strategic plans. Main themes include:

1 Total number of student enrolments funded by the council is expected to reach 3.1 million by 1996–7, an increase of 21 per cent from 1993–4. (see tables 2.1–2.4).
2 The Secretary of State's target of overall expansion of 25 per cent should be achieved by 1996–7.
3 No significant changes are projected in the balance of provision between programme areas or mode of study and no major withdrawal of provisions planning in any programme area.

4   The principal risks to the achievement of college objectives are identified as increasing competition particularly from school sixth forms and
the availability of student support.

In 1993–94, 9 per cent of full-time enrolments in colleges were wholly
funded from sources other than the council. This includes provision funded
by the Higher Education Funding Council in England in further education
sector colleges, Employment Department funded schemes and full-cost
recovery programmes.

The increase in full-time enrolments funded from other sources is projected to be 16 per cent up to 1996–97. The increase in part-time enrolments
is expected to be 6 per cent up to 1996–97.

Table 2.1   Council-funded provision in further education colleges

	1993–1994	1996–1997
Full time	648	798
Part time	1,567	1,885
	2,215	2,683

Table 2.2   Enrolments in colleges (full time)

1993–4 Programme area	FE colleges Enrolment	%	Sixth-form colleges Enrolment	%	Programme area
Sciences	61,803	12	29,480	30	Sciences
Construction	19,926	4	0	0	Construction
Engineering	48,816	9	890	1	Engineering
Business	86,435	16	9,813	10	Business
Hotel and catering	51,266	10	1,575	2	Hotel and catering
Health and community care	78,162	15	2,170	2	Health and community care
Art and design	56,687	11	9,815	10	Art and design
Humanities	115,363	22	45,470	46	Humanities
Basic education	11,756	2	661	1	Basic education
Total	530,214	100	99,874	100	Total

Percentages may not add to totals due to rounding

Table 2.3 Enrolments in colleges (part time)

1993–4 Programme area	FE colleges Enrolment	%	Sixth-form colleges Enrolment	%	Programme area
Sciences	146,203	10	2,909	19	Sciences
Construction	73,488	5	0	0	Construction
Engineering	179,121	12	264	2	Engineering
Business	312,701	20	2,380	21	Business
Hotel and catering	44,866	3	80	1	Hotel and catering
Health and community care	102,929	7	637	6	Health and community care
Art and design	71,957	5	0	0	Care
Humanities	460,210	30	679	6	Art and design
Basic education	130,051	8	4,233	37	Humanities
			957	8	Basic education
Total	1,521,526	100	99,874	100	Total

Table 2.4 Higher education provision in further education colleges franchised from higher education institutions

Programme area	1993–4 Enrolments	1996–7 Enrolments Projected
Sciences	4,172	6,691
Agriculture	1,519	2,469
Construction	1,032	1,629
Engineering	2,943	5,005
Business	6,151	7,200
Hotel and catering	2,612	3,269
Health and community care	1,220	2,034
Art and design	2,705	4,402
Humanities	2,922	3,590
Basic education	0	0
Total	25,276	36,289

Appendix 2.3: Cleveland College Franchises for Mainstream Non-advanced Further Education

The broad categories of provision of vocational education and training currently made at each college is set out below. These categories are not intended to be an exhaustive guide to the courses each college offers. However, they do give some indication of the courses and subject areas available in the colleges.

Cleveland College of Art and Design (based in Middlesbrough)

Art and design; printing and decorating (shared with Hartlepool College).

Cleveland Technical College (based in Redcar)

Building and civil engineering technician courses; building trades; music.

Secretarial/clerical; intermediate management; computer applications; electrical/electronic engineering; general engineering; pre-nursing; fabrication and welding; family and community care.

Hartlepool College of Further Education

Building and civil engineering technical courses; building trades; professional computing and IT courses; motor vehicle repair and maintenance; electrical installation.

Secretarial/clerical; intermediate management; computer applications; supervisory studies; trade union studies; hairdressing and beauty culture; pre-nursing; family and community care; mechanical and production engineering; electrical and electronic engineering; plant maintenance; fabrication and welding.

Kirby College of Further Education (based in Middlesbrough)

Catering; social care work; hairdressing (except Hartlepool) and beauty therapy; Institute of Linguists Foreign Languages; leisure and recreation (joint with Longlands College); Teaching English as a Foreign Language (TEFL).

Secretarial/clerical; intermediate management; computer applications, pre-nursing; financial/legal/accounting courses.

Longlands College of Further Education (based in Middlesbrough)

Telecommunications; salesmanship; leisure and recreation (joint with Kirby College); industrial measurement and process control; heating and ventilation.

Audio-visual aids; motor vehicle repair and maintenance; security alarms; electrical installation; professional computing and IT courses; science; quality assurance; non-destructive testing.

Computer applications; trade union studies; electrical and electronic engineering; general engineering; plant maintenance; fabrication and welding.

Stockton and Billingham Technical College

Trade union safety representatives courses; nursery nursing courses; teacher training; electronic serving; equitation; performing and creative arts; construction plant engineering.

Music, audio-visual aids; security alarms; science; quality assurance; non-destructive testing.

Secretarial/clerical; pre-nursing; family and community care; trade union studies; electrical and electronic engineering; general engineering; plant maintenance; mechanical and production engineering; fabrication and welding.

3

Strategic Change in Local Government Management – Comparative Case Studies*

ALAN LAWTON AND DAVID MCKEVITT

This case study examines how organizations seek to respond to changes in their external environment through the development of strategies which match organizational capability with external constraints. It is concerned with how organizations implement change. The case is concerned with how strategic change is both facilitated and constrained by the relationship between the organization and its environment.

The case reports on local authority changes in three authorities – a rural district council in the South of England (hereafter Westchester), Tilburg City Council in Holland and Cologne City Council in Germany.

Westchester District Council

The debate on the future of local government as the provider of local services in the United Kingdom has centered on the idea of the enabling authority, with the role of the centre seen as the strategic management of service delivery through partnerships and contracts with external private, voluntary and not-for-profit organizations. Local authorities have faced a turbulent environment, legislative, economic and political, and have been

* The case draws upon interviews with senior managers, clients and consultants involved with the three authorities.

encouraged to adopt more 'business-like' approaches to the management of service delivery. The concept of the enabling authority, together with the theme of responsiveness to the citizen/client, has become part of the basic framework for the strategic management of local authorities.

Westchester is a rural district authority based in the South of England. In response to the financial constraints facing local authorities in the UK throughout the 1980s, the authority responded by introducing a system of cost centres to assist in the management of its service delivery. The impetus behind the restructuring into cost centres was officer driven, albeit with broad political support. As the Chief Executive put it: 'I did have the advantage that the members have realized that they wanted to effect change and so I had good support from the members at an early stage.'

The initiative, begun in 1989, was primarily seen as a response to the external financial environment and it was an organization-wide process, involving the redesign of some 180 cost centres. While the centre was instrumental in initiating the change, management adopted what they considered to be an 'umbrella' strategy (defined as originating in constraints the boundaries of which are defined by the leadership within which managers operate. The environment is often unpredictable) to the redesign of cost centres which was the responsibility of the individual service areas. The change process was an incremental one – 'We learned by trial and error' – and such an approach is seen in the Environmental Health Services in reducing its number of cost centres from 23 to 13 and, in 1992, to 11.

Westchester responded to the demands of external environment through its Customer Charter. This was put in place at the beginning of 1991 and sets out service levels and targets and gives details of contact points for comments and complaints. It also carried out a Residents Attitude Survey in 1991.

Development of cost centres

The content (the 'what') of change concerned the use of cost centres. The case illustrates the impact of cost centres in two divisions of the authority, Environmental Health Services where much of the work is driven by statute, and in Community and Leisure Services where much of the work is discretionary.

Cost centres were described as 'transferable technology', i.e. the approach did not depend on which political party was in power. Indeed, there appeared to be general support among the politicians for the changes. (In mid-1991

Lib Dems took control from the Conservatives.) There appeared to be broad agreement on the authority's strategy:

> I think that within most authorities members do work for the good of the community and many of the things that one party would tackle, the other parties would have to tackle. One example is homelessness, which is a key issue here.

Politicians were encouraged to take a more strategic role and there was a view that cost centres encouraged this development.

Cost centres, also described as localized budgeting, were structured as a collection of expenditure areas linked to service activities. In Environmental Health, cost centres were designed around the following criteria: statutory or non-statutory, commercial or non-commercial, food hygiene or safety, and in terms of the inspection processes involved. In Community and Leisure Services cost centres were focused on the following policy areas: key client groups, arts development and small one-off grants. In the words of one senior manager, cost centres assisted in the clarification of management tasks: 'It gives them (managers) boundaries, it gives them responsibilities, and it gives them clarity of purpose.' However, as one manager put it:

> Given that the field of leisure is a discretionary service, it does give you extra freedom. You are not bound by having to carry out food inspections or having to carry out certain elements of the service.

The devolution of responsibility for service provision through the cost centre approach has meant that managers can exercise some discretion in budgetary allocation. In Environmental Health approximately 80 per cent of costs are associated with salaries, some 6 per cent is spent on central services, leaving 14 per cent where some element of discretion can be exercised. As important as the amount available for discretionary spending is the perception by managers that they have some control over spending decisions. Awareness of financial costs, it is argued, makes the manager more effective. A community development manager reported that:

> Financial awareness of budgeting and control of that process makes me more effective in community development work than a manager who didn't have that degree of control and who fell into the trap of going round and promising things that budgets couldn't deliver.

Similarly, in environmental health:

> Under the old system the chief environmental health officer would have had
> the major say in any expenditure and the second-tier officers would follow
> out those orders. Now, cost centre managers are totally responsible for their
> budget and hopefully take more interest in the job.

A dissenting voice expressed the view that:

> To an extent there are variables which are beyond our control – salaries, for
> example. There are central charges which are fixed. We are moving to
> service level agreements with the centre where these charges are negotiated.

The process of change management

The process of change is facilitated through a number of sub-processes.
The co-ordination of cost centres is managed through business plans which
include performance targets that are also used as a focus for accountability.
In Environmental Health, for example, some targets are derived from
legislation such as the requirement to periodically review food premises, or
by the customer in the form of complaints. In Community Development,
specific targets are set in terms of usage of community centres, the number
of parishes within which community development takes place or in processing
new applications for grant aid. There is an acceptance that, in community
development work, targets are not always easy to set and quantify.

Monitoring through target setting characterizes the relationship between
the Westchester Council and outside bodies. In community development
the authority supports groups on a trial basis and then moves to a more
business-like approach with its key client groups. A three-year plan is
agreed between the key client group and the authority with expenditure
monitored on a monthly basis. The authority offers advice to key client
groups and encourages such groups to develop their own targets and strategy. A voluntary group that manages a community centre has been encouraged to take on the management of a second centre. Key client groups
have more financial security than with an annual grant and are encouraged
to take a step back from day-to-day problems and adopt a more strategic
perspective. The business plan has prompted key client groups to look at
the sort of services it wants to offer, and can afford to offer, to the local
community.

Westchester has also used cost centres to encourage partnerships. Managers are encouraged to be innovative and to seek new opportunities to

develop the 'seamless divide' between the authority and the community. In the case of community groups:

> Our managers don't go in once a year and give grants, they live and work with these people seven nights a week ... We want to work within the community where ideas emerge even if we are not there and ultimately the end product is what matters, not who achieved it and how it is achieved ... We are encouraging much greater interaction [so] that the strengths of individual groups can be passed on to other groups so that the wheel does not have to be reinvented every time.

In Environmental Health the relationship with outside bodies has been put on a more commercial basis. Managers are encouraged to be entrepreneurial and to seek opportunities for income generation. An example of such entrepreneurial activity is the training given to commercial organizations on food hygiene and legislation concerning food safety. Costs centres have allowed for realistic prices to be charged for services which reflect the costs involved. Hitherto, not all costs were taken into account.

For this Authority a cost centre approach and the enabling authority are interlinked. One senior manager argued:

> I don't think a traditional style of centrally led accountancy-based local authority management would lead to an enabling authority. I think the two, the cost centre approach with clear targets and objectives, and the enabling authority, go hand in hand.

Westchester is developing Service Level Agreements between the cost centres and the central services so that the cost of support services such as personnel or accounting is transparent. As one manager put it:

> If we get to that stage, where I have a greater degree of control over the level of service and thereby the level of costs charged to me by central administration, then I'll feel that we have properly got cost centre managements.

The change process has not been easy. Typical responses to the issue of change were:

> I don't think there was any one major resistance, I think some people were frightened to take on board the responsibility whether or not they had the skills and the knowledge to do the work.

When professionals were told that they were fully in charge of a service and they couldn't rely on other people to do it for them, it was quite a shock.

I don't think you ever fully achieve cultural change because the next change is around the corner.

Management development started with some 70 senior managers undertaking training on cultural change and then more specific training on financial management, policy review and performance review. The intensive training programme, which lasted for almost one year, relied on managers' capacity to absorb change processes. The Chief Executive indicated that:

In fact, in retrospect, I think it was too intensive; we expected them to take on too many things too quickly. Not only convince them that the future with the organization lay in the 'Way Ahead' as we called it, but we had to give them the basic skills of manpower and financial responsibility in a very short space of time. I think that what we did was to overload one or two of them, but the ones that could take it on board were the ones that actually succeeded.

Some senior managers were redeployed prior to the changes because it was perceived that they would be unable to cope with the new demands placed on them. Different departments followed their own route to the design of cost centres. However, cost centre management (the content of strategic change) has, it was argued, facilitated management in the clarification of their tasks, and it has allowed for greater participation with some service users, particularly in community services.

Politician–manager relations

The process of decision making, top down, together with the speed of change implementation, has given rise to difficulty in the politician–manager interface and the ability of managers and politicians to absorb the scope of the proposed changes. Different perspectives are reflected in the following quotes:

I represent the public and I see cost centre management as enabling me to perform the role more effectively. If we can provide services more efficiently and effectively, everybody gains.

I think that the larger the organization the more professional the staff and the greater the tendency for the management team to pull away more and more day-to-day power from elected members and to run the service and to come to members once a year in the budget process and say, these are the ideas that we have got will you give us the authority and the finance to do that?

I would accept that some members see it as a threat [devolved responsibility to managers] but if you have got the right rapport between the officers and the members there is no danger as long as everybody recognizes that they do have limits which they should not overstep the mark.

I think the important thing is members ought to be looking at the overall policies and looking at the strategic aims and not getting too bogged down with some of the itsy-bitsy detail.

We have to let the officers get on with the day-to-day running of the authority. That is what they are there for. We should be trying to steer and I hope we do steer in the direction that we originally set out in our manifesto.

Leading politicians were involved in the decision to develop cost centres and saw the need for them to become more involved in the strategic direction of the Authority, but backbench politicians had difficulty in adjusting to the changes. As far as the managers were concerned a number of different viewpoints was expressed:

Our local authority introduced some management training because it real-ized that people like myself who've been in local government for many years needed managerial skills adding to our professional skills. Cost centres have made us use those management skills.

In the old days of local government, the professional could broadly say this is my profession and this is the way we should go. We underestimated how difficult the transition from being a professional to a manager would be.

We did a vision-changing seminar for all members of staff so at least they had an idea of the cultural change we were going through. We also had specific training on things like financial management, policy review, per-formance review so that they actually got some management training. I think the first phase of group training went quite well but I think that, perhaps, we could have done more on the personal training.

Previously managers had seen themselves as part of a democratic organi-zation. Cost centre management has made them think of themselves as small

business managers and why should they be part of a democratic organization. Well, local authorities are democratic organizations and they have to
bear their share of the costs.

I have held the view for many years that if you let people get on with an idea
and give them a real sense of empowerment, they won't let you down.

It is quite often the trivia that gives the vision a human face. None of us
could spend all our time up there in the clouds looking at the grand vision.

The City of Tilburg

In Holland the role of government as the sole provider of services has been
challenged. At local level, municipalities have been encouraged to enter
into networks and partnerships with other organizations including those in
the private and voluntary sectors. As a unitary state, central government in
Holland has had a strong role to play in formulating policy but powers
of general competence have allowed local municipalities to respond to
local characteristics. (Appendix 3.1 gives background information on Dutch
local authorities.) However, funding is through, primarily, central government specific grants. Local municipalities have been encouraged to be more
businesslike in their activities and to concentrate on performance outputs
rather than inputs.

Politician–manager relations

Tilburg, in common with Westchester, faced financial constraints in the
mid-1980s when it began its process of strategic change. The impetus for
change was shared between the politicians and officers and it was prompted
by the questions 'What are we doing and are we doing it well for the
citizens of Tilburg?' From the outset the politicians had the primary role
in directing strategy and in the creation of information systems which
would assist political direction. Politicians perceived that the new system would provide them with a competence in directing the scope of the
organization's activity, and management clearly acknowledged the primacy
of political decision making. As the Chief Executive put it:

Modern managers often try to achieve optimum management and consider
political interventions, originating from another system of values, a nui-
sance. But they should also be capable of judging the political aspects of a

case correctly and take them up actively, without disclaiming their own outlook on management for that matter. Whoever is unable to accept this, should not become an administrative manager.

The impact on politicians has been significant. According to one senior manager:

> The politicians wanted to go back to 'what?' question and the managers wanted to get rid of the politicians in the 'how?' question. And that is the game we have played, giving back the power to the politicians in deciding what has to be done and in return we have freedom to create a situation in which we could do what was wanted for our customers.

There is some disagreement about the appropriate role for politicians, however:

> Management say you have to get more involved with the outlines [strategy]. Well, that is OK, but citizens are not interested in outlines, they are interested in what is happening in their own street, what is happening with housing, environment and so on.

> I think that local government is in a kind of crisis in terms of political ideology because there are so many things which we deliver as a city which really aren't an issue in political discussion. The citizen is sitting there seeing this discussion and thinking what the hell are they talking about? It is not a political issue.

The implementation of what has become known as the 'Tilburg model' was facilitated by financial and information systems redesign. The authority did not know how money was being spent or how effective it was in delivering its services. The approach has been described by one of its architects as 'New Realism' and focuses upon decentralization and delegation, professional management and political control with respect to strategy.

The content of reform included organizational structure and organizational culture; information systems and the allocation of financial accountability; the quality of management and the development of competences. Key elements of the process are the decentralization of structures and the delegation of responsibility; the use of business management techniques and contract management and the focus on outputs rather than inputs. And yet:

Sometimes it is very difficult for people working in government to understand that they are making something. In Tilburg there was a lot of energy invested in defining products and making clear what cost could be attributed to those products.

It is very difficult to measure the social effects of what you are doing.

The budget is linked to performance (input to output) and the focus is customer oriented.

Structural Change

Structural changes were accompanied by radical redeployment of staff; some 1,000 employees were redeployed in the new system and the size of the central department was reduced (over some seven years) from 350 to 30 staff. While the scope of the changes were organization-wide, Tilburg explicitly adopted what was defined as an emergent strategy – 'because we didn't realize when we started where we should end' – and it did not perceive any significant benefits from its organizational change until three years after initiation in 1985. This contrasts with Westchester where a rapid reorganization was applied without giving due concern to the internal processes required to support it.

The provision of central services is now the responsibility of a separate department which competes with outside bodies in the provision of, for example, legal services. The centre has a network relationship with the line departments. According to one senior officer, 'This is how value is added'. The line departments have become semi-autonomous. The role of the centre now is to support the political system, develop a central strategy, and co-ordinate the operation of the line departments through standards and targets. The performance targets set by the politicians act as the focus for operational control.

A central feature of strategic control is the development of service outputs and delivery targets the content of change. Different stakeholders are involved in the setting of the targets; politicians, managers and the customers. The explicit involvement of service users is key to the Tilburg change process and derives from Tilburg's initial strategic impetus which was directed at its citizen/consumer. The Tilburg Passport Office aims to deliver a passport in 15 minutes. The managers asked the customers what they thought was an acceptable waiting time and changed the delivery systems to meet that target.

The relationship with the voluntary sector is also structured by target setting. Money can be retained if the organization proves to be more efficient. The system encourages the clients to be proactive in their internal management. Targets are negotiated with politicians and managers and monitored by the council; managers can lose their jobs if targets are not met. According to one senior manager, 'That was the main change; we are now much more interested in the outputs than the processes (of the budget system)'.

There has been a shift from input to output control, specifying output in terms of quantity, quality and customer requirements and determining the price, standards and characteristics of performance. The difficulty in defining targets is recognized; in the first instance there are those services that are quantifiable such as turnaround times on passports; secondly, extensive use is made of consumer survey panels to ascertain customer satisfaction. The Council also recognizes that it has to explore how to measure outcomes in terms of the social effects of its services on the community.

Determining strategic objectives

Tilburg attended to the 'how' of change, to the processes involved in strategic change; relations between politicians and managers were seen as crucial to the successful implementation of change. In Tilburg the elected municipal council elects from its own members the municipal board which acts as the executive; agreed strategy is determined by the council, and the board reports to it once a year on progress, whereby adjustments are made to the strategic direction. The management report (MARAP) whereby the departmental heads reports to the council and the municipal board three times a year on the progress of the departmental budget, was described by one politician as 'an early alarm system'.

Relations between the line departments and the council are structured by contracts described as 'gentleman's agreements'. The director of a department makes a contract with the town council, the politicians; a contract is also made with his or her profit centre managers. The contract relationship thus works to integrate the political and operational management of the council.

A problem for politicians is that constituents may not be interested in long-term strategy but more interested in the quality of existing services and they expect their politician to be accountable. City councillors seek to balance the need to develop strategy and to be aware of the details of their constituents' interest. As one politician put it:

It is a dilemma. I think that city councillors will have to do their best to also get involved in details and to see that achievements match the outlines of strategy.

To give up control of operational matters to managers requires trust and a culture of openness:

You have to have mutual trust, between managers and city councillors, and also between city councillors themselves. Perhaps that is something special about Dutch politics, which is a compromise politics.

Traditionally the manager:

was very concerned with his own department and he tried to sweep his own floor clean and move the dirt to his neighbour. The new manager needs more entrepreneurial qualities, he is more interested in the goals of the city as a whole, even if it costs something to his own department.

The development of managers has focused on the acquisition of skills in communication and business techniques. This contrasts with 1985 when the background of managers tended to be administrative/legal. Managers now require different skills:

Reaching a goal is more important than doing your own job, you have to be interested in goals and products and not in processes. You also have to be an open social person with an open mind to everybody else. You have to be an entrepreneur in that respect;

and,

It is not a manager with a legislative background that we need but a business manager with a commercial background that is more important.

Attention to the scope of institutional and technical change was captured by the Chief Executive

laying down political standards and index numbers for management performance is one of the great challenges of the 1990s in the Netherlands.

Cologne

The federal nature of the German State encourages diverse and complex relations between the different levels of government. Local authorities are essentially autonomous in their taxing powers and generally are heavily reliant on local businesses taxes. A fluctuating economy and the costs of unification have had major impacts on the finances of local authorities.

Within local authorities there is a tradition of strong executive control. Local authorities have traditionally acted as providers of local services with a limited involvement with partners, and a competitive model has not been widely used. (Appendix 3.2 provides background on German local government.)

Cologne City Council adopted a top-down, officer-led strategy to organizational change. The geographical proximity of Tilburg provided Cologne with a framework for strategic change, although it was acknowledged that the political, managerial and legal environment of Germany would preclude any direct adoption of the Tilburg model. The economic context was broadly similar to that of Tilburg and of Westchester, i.e. the need to constrain the costs of service delivery; in Cologne, 'The main objective is to achieve at least the same effect by using fewer resources'. At the same time, senior managers felt that, to win political support, reforms have to be seen to save money as well as guaranteeing better services for their voters.

Senior managers in Cologne clearly identified the internal organizational context, with its legal character, of German local government as a constraint on any large-scale change. German local authorities are characterized by a uniform structure with clearly specified functional divisions and with strong central control. Local government is strongly regulated through laws and regulations. The development of managerial skills has been hampered by a strict division of labour with little stress on entrepreneurial skills. As one commentator put it:

> Well, the managers of today in the local authorities as in other public authorities, they are trained to execute laws, to guarantee equity before the law and to exercise the rules.

Devolved budgeting is not common and authorities tend to be oriented towards inputs and processes rather than outputs and outcomes. Responsiveness is seen as less important than legality, economy and efficiency although consumer rights are traditionally represented in law. In Cologne there was little evidence of the expansion of consumer choice. In order to bring about change, one commentator argued that:

> You first have to convince politicians and staff that you have got a problem you cannot solve in the traditional way and within the old system. Then you have to stimulate a learning process of all the important actors that they have an interest in changing the organization and their own behaviour.

Cologne has adopted a deliberate approach to change and has established business units in two pilot areas, traffic control and garbage disposal, giving managers greater control over resources. The content of change is, therefore, not dissimiliar to the other two cases. Senior managers considered that these two departments – traffic control and garbage disposal – lend themselves to the creation of business units and financial systems were well established in these areas. It was also believed that traffic control is appropriate for a more responsive approach since traffic wardens can be used as front-line managers to get closer to the customer! In principle it was indicated that 90 per cent of Cologne's activities could be carried out through business units. However, in practice this may prove difficult to achieve:

> It is a big problem because the nightmare of the bureaucrats today is that this [the move to business units] will all end in anarchy. This is especially the nightmare of the persons responsible for the central functions such as personnel and finance. They are afraid that they will lose control to autonomous business units.

The strong role of the central departments of finance, personnel and central organization may, however, constrain moves to greater autonomy for line departments. The context of change may be too restricted to have any significant impact on changing the internal culture of the organization or in effecting change processes in the organization as a whole. Changes involve: giving the pilot areas responsibility not just for technical responsibilities and for personnel and finance; greater flexibility for new working hours and recruitment of staff; decentralization and more control over targets for service delivery. Managers expressed their scepticism:

> The pilot study may be too small. The responsibility for all the resources like personnel and finance means that you have to decentralize your central personnel or your finance departments and you can't do that on a scale which is too small because there is nothing to decentralize.

And traditionally:

> Decentralized control over resources very often takes the form that the head of central finance cuts the budget of the department and leaves it to the head of the department where to save the money.

In describing Cologne's change strategy one manager stated that:

> Cologne is one of the few authorities with a vision of where it wants to go. It is at the start of the process and we should not compare it with Tilburg which is much further down the road.

These changes require managers to develop new skills. Managers in pilot projects find the stress on individual responsibility and accountability difficult. 'In the past it was easy to pass on responsibility by arguing that there was not enough money, not enough personnel, the wrong people, another office is responsible.' And yet, 'A lot of the managers in the old system found it frustrating not to be able to put their ideas into practice.'

The need for changes in management culture was recognized by one local government adviser:

> Traditionally managers in our local authorities, they are rather perfectionists. They are living in the perfect system of the nineteenth century and would rather wait for the next perfect solution before they start to change. We have to ensure cultural change. It will not happen overnight. It is easy to change structures but this is not enough. . . . You also have to ensure that the personnel are able to fulfil the new tasks so you need a lot of training and education.

In contrasting Cologne with Tilburg one commentator stated that:

> In my eyes the reform movement in the Netherlands can give us many fruitful ideas, concepts and examples of change. We can learn from their experiences, from their improvements and from the mistakes that they have made. But German cities have to find their own way. They have to solve their own problems and not the ones of Tilburg or other Dutch cities.

One problem is that of context:

> There are obstacles on the legal side. Many laws have to be changed and adapted to the new management tools. In Germany we still have a rather big split between the public sector with its many many rules and legislation and laws and the private sector.

Discussion Questions

1 How successful were the three authorities in changing the internal context and processes to respond to the external environment?

2 Does giving managers greater responsibility take away from the democratic process?

3 Were the human resource strategies adopted in each authority appropriate to the organizational changes?

4 How meaningful is it to make comparisons between different local authorities?

Appendix 3.1: Key Features of Local Government in Holland

- The municipality is the basic form of local government in Holland.
- There are approximately 700 in number, each with local autonomy.
- They have powers of general competence so that they can carry out any activity that is not regulated by regional or national government.
- There is some local taxation but 90 per cent of financing comes from central government general and specific grants.
- There is bargaining between the different layers of government and coalition politics and co-operative ventures are a way of life.
- Direct elections take place every four years and elect between 7–45 council members depending on the size of the municipality.

The municipal executive is the core of local government and is made up of a mayor, appointed by central government, and two to six members of the council elected by their fellow members.

Appendix 3.2: Key Features of Local Government in Germany

- Germany has a federal system of government.
- The most basic level of government is at local level and consists of counties and county-free cities and below them the municipalities.
- There are approximately 8,500 counties and municipalities.
- Intergovernmental co-operation between the different layers of government is normal.
- There is a power of general competence.
- Local income taxes raise 30 per cent of local government expenditure.
- There is a tradition of strong executive government.
- Direct elections choose between 20–80 members in the counties which appoint their own executive of between 5–12 members.

4

Light at the End of the Tunnel

PAUL KETCHLEY AND PIERRE MONGIN

Closer contacts between the UK, France and the rest of Europe have been symbolized by the construction of the Channel Tunnel which opened in 1994 for freight and subsequently passenger traffic. However, alongside the development of major infrastructure projects there has been an increasing co-operation and joint working by public services on both sides of the Channel. This has brought a realization of the common developments in the management of public services in France and the UK and, as well as the common themes, there has been a realization of the differences and diversity in the approaches to public service management.

This case examines these developments, their origin and the institutional changes they have brought about. The case looks at the the impact of devolution and decentralization in both England and France and the impact on the management task, and assesses the issues which now face managers in local government on both sides of the Channel. The case focuses on the work of two senior managers in local government in France and in England. Gilles Amaudric du Chaffaut is Deputy Chief Executive responsible for Social Policy and Affairs at the Pas de Calais Departement, based in Arras around 50 miles south of the French exit of the tunnel. The case also examines the experience of David McGahey, Head of Customer and Community Services in the Education Department of Kent County Council in Maidstone, who is about 25 miles from the UK tunnel exit at Cheriton near Folkestone.

Both managers have long and successful careers in public services in their country. As a result they have both seen and experienced the changes in public service management brought about over the past ten years by a Conservative government in Britain and by a Socialist government in France. These changes can be grouped into a number of common themes. These are:

- devolution and decentralization to locally accountable groups;
- the shift from an administrative to a managerial culture;
- a greater 'intrusion' of politics into management;
- an increasingly complex managerial environment.

Devolution and Decentralization

In both the UK and in France devolution and decentralization have been common themes over the past 20 years. Indeed, in France the need to decentralize was recognized in the 1960s but not implemented formally until the enactment of the 1982 law of decentralization.

The nature of devolution has, perhaps inevitably, been very different. In England there has been a devolution of authority, and particularly for financial management, away from the centre of local authorities and out to services. In the case of schools this has meant the delegation of very significant funds and power to make decisions on a whole range of issues from local authorities (LEAs) down to the level of the school itself. It has also meant the introduction of quasi market-based purchaser–provider relationships where money for common services has been passed out to schools for them to 'buy back' the services which they value the most. Functions have also passed out of the local authority to autonomous public corporations funded from central government agencies on a formula funding basis.

In France there have been similar changes as whole new tiers of local government have been created at regional level, and functions previously held by the agencies of central government or the State and operated on a local basis by an administrative bureaucracy headed by the prefect have been transferred to the control of the *départements*. As part of the process there has been a series of major changes for the local authorities designated to oversee the delivery of services, particularly the *départements*, which have become the major service-providing tier of French local government outside the larger towns and cities. Appendix 4.1 provides details of the changes.

In both countries the formal shifts of power and resources directly affected local authority structures. In England the power of local education authorities to promulgate common policies has been significantly reduced through the introduction of schemes of local management of schools and the 'peeling off' of functions to other agencies. This latter approach has meant the transfer out of local government of the former polytechnics, the colleges of further education and sixth-form colleges, and the opting out of a number of schools, mainly in the secondary sector, to grant maintained (GM) status. The careers service has been transferred out of the control of the local authority and is now effectively an arms-length service delivered under contract to central government. In France, by contrast, there have been significant shifts of resources and responsibilities out of central government and into local agencies. Seventy-five per cent of the employees of the Department of Health and Social Affairs, (DASS), have been transferred out to work in the *départements*, which are now far more accountable for the delivery of services and for local financial management. This has meant the transfer of staff out of the mainstream civil service and into local government organizations. In the case of the Pas de Calais, with a population of 1.5 million, this has meant the absorbtion of around 1,800 staff.

Similar changes have resulted in France from the devolution of agencies from central government. Control passed from the prefect, who was the local representative of the State, not unlike the governor–general in the British colonial system, to the expanded *départements* and the new generation of *élus*, the elected members (*conseillers générals*) who now manage the services provided by these agencies. As a result a new managerial approach has been required in France at local level:

> I think it all started with the new type of elected councillor we have begun to see since 1977 or so. They wanted to operate more independently and so they took on more able people and you had a general process of improving the qualifications people had and also of better management. This was particularly so amongst the larger towns and cities. This meant that they had the management tools to carry out projects and improve their performance. Decentralisation simply accentuated the whole process. You got financial managers in place locally and that gave you a managerial basis on which to carry out projects and that lead on to the improved management of human resources.

In France the key change experienced by Gilles du Chaffaut was the introduction of new political and administrative structures which brought in a new generation of elected politicians at local level:

> Decentralisation really built on changes which had been going on for some time. With the new local politicians who had been in place since 1977 you had people with a more managerial approach . . . they had wanted to get away from the administrative role for some time anyway, the supervision of the State and all the technical oversight. I remember that we took on a technical manager in my authority and the outcry that caused in the DDE

(the local outpost of the Ministry of Works). . . . when we started to set up
our own projects . . . only small ones mind you. . . . because we showed that
we were capable of setting them up and managing them ourselves and as a
result we were not paying the management fees to the DDE as we had
previously had to do.

There has, however, been a major difference in approach. In England
there has been a process of separating functions from the local government
base leading to the loss of an integrated local framework for service provision, particularly for planning and integration. Many institutions are funded
directly from central government and can act independently and often in
their own interests. The justification for this approach has been expressed
in the form of the need for choice and increased responsiveness. Few
would argue that initiatives to promote local management have not been
beneficial; however, there is great concern about measures which have led
to the break-up of local planning frameworks. Central to this argument has
been the creation of a significant grant-maintained sector of schools and the
peeling off of further education functions and sixth-form colleges from
local authority control. David McGahey describes it from his point of view:

> On the whole, the changes out there and the way they have impacted on the
> role of the Education Manager have been largely beneficial. It is no longer
> possible to go on being what I was describing earlier as an old-fashioned
> Education Officer operating within a command economy type environment.
> Whether or not the changes have been in the interest of the Education and
> Training service as a whole, I'm a lot less sure about that. I'm not at all sure
> that the more fragmented environment in which we are now operating is
> delivering what our country needs. There are some real issues in terms of
> schools not working together, colleges and schools not working together and
> there are some real gaps emerging between institutions and organisations
> into which people are increasingly falling. The balance is increasingly wrong
> between the proper devolution of responsibilities to schools and colleges and
> the need to maintain some sort of framework not just at national but also at
> local level. I think we've lost the local framework which brings about local
> coherence in policy, strategy formulation and service delivery, and we are
> going to regret this fairly soon. It makes it very difficult to achieve what
> central government wants to do at local level. I was talking to a senior
> businessman recently who was saying that if you want to achieve change it's
> ludicrous to fragment your resource streams in the way central government
> has done in the last few years.

Critics argue that the policy imperative of increasing parental choice is
actually being experienced by parents as one in which there is less and less

choice as schools, and particularly those in the grant maintained sector in which the school has control of its admission arrangements, are determining their own admissions criteria. Parents find that effective choice lies with the school. In the field of vocational training, generally seen as a national priority, David McGahey argues that:

> There is increasing competition between schools and colleges and they are tripping over themselves in the hunt to recruit pupils and students post 16. There is also fragmentation between providers of education and providers of training and so at a local level now we are having to find ways round that by creating collaboration between the TEC, the County Council, and trying to bring into that Further Education Colleges, schools, private training providers and so on. Now as anybody knows who has worked in public sector, and for the private sector for that matter, it is very much more difficult to do that where you are all working in different organisations without the same framework or strategy than if you work in a single organisation or framework, in fact it's difficult enough in a single organisation when you are trying to bring together a whole range of interests with a variety of agendas and styles.

Similar issues of integration are being experienced in France but from a different point of view. Many of the services which have been decentralized have historically worked on different geographical boundaries to one another. This has led the *départements* to question the way in which they should deliver these services at a local level and the relationships between services. However, the fact that they all operate within the same organizational structure has greatly increased the ability to achieve a co-ordinated approach.

> In the Pas de Calais we inherited a system called the Health and Social Service Districts which was set up in 1964 and which was an organization with its own geographical boundaries. We are going to have to rethink and to restructure the whole thing because it does not relate to the boundaries of all the other services, especially in the urban areas. This in turn got us thinking in terms of multi-purpose local integration of services and I think that all French *départements* are thinking about how to achieve this. It's really important to ensure that we get this multi-purpose approach down to a local level. It made us think about local delivery of services and so the Pas de Calais Département has been one of the leaders in setting up local offices which we call '*antennes locales*' and we really have to think through their role, how they relate to the local services provided by communes, local councillors and the sub-prefectorial offices.

Administration to Management

In both countries a major spur to change was the dominance of an administrative approach within their public services. This was described by David McGahey as follows:

> There was a direct managerial relationship then between schools and further education colleges and the local authority. It was possible to promote common policies in a more straightforward fashion than arguably it is at the moment, and it was possible to bring about what might be described as a mini-revolution in some services, not that I think most local education authorities made the most of these opportunities. My feeling at that time, 10 or 12 years ago, was that what we had then in LEAs was much too much of an administrative rather than a managerial culture. Although we did a lot to try to break out of that I think there were still greater developments that we could have brought about and I think that in general we did not make the most of the potential available to us at that time.

Now, David McGahey argues:

> Funnily enough, there is an extent to which things haven't changed, although they have become a good deal more difficult. What I've seen is an increasing managerialism in the way in which LEAs and institutions within them work together. We have become, at its crudest, less administrative and more managerial. There is a more balanced relationship now and not least as a result of local management. Changing times have meant that the Education Service needs to be more responsive and on occasions more proactive in taking a leadership role. At the same time there has been a much greater maturity in schools, in their ability to manage themselves, and this in turn has required a change in culture in LEAs where I think that, by and large, people have changed their style of working considerably over the last ten years. That has been a good preparation for the situation now where we work in a much more disparate education and training community. It means that we are much better set up to cope with the much more complex environment in which we are now all working.

As a result there has been a complete change in culture brought about in local authorities on both sides of the Channel. Ways of working have had to change and there has been an influx of new people with a wider range of backgrounds. In the search for greater organizational effectiveness there has been a growing focus on service delivery. Particularly in France, where civil servants have been transferred to organizations involved in service delivery, this has been a very significant change and one which is still being addressed.

In France the change in culture has been more difficult to achieve since the requirement was not to adapt an existing organization but to integrate a very large number of national civil servants into local service providing agencies and ensuring that these were not simply administrative bureaucracies. From Gilles du Chaffaut's perspective:

> Financial devolution might simply have turned us into a counting-house. I thought from the staff point of view it was really important to integrate these people into the *départements* little by little, whatever their specializations. None of them has the same culture and some seemed to lack a service culture at all, and that's the real challenge, it's to bring all these people into a shared culture. At the moment they don't have that really positive service view that you find, say, in the larger towns and city communes, they think they are above all that, but in fact they are way behind. It's a very general thing and perhaps it is a hangover from the culture of the prefects office which they have brought with them. It's a feeling of 'superiority', which needs to be put in inverted commas because you can't put your finger on it in the methods of management but strangely enough you see it in the administrative processes, how files get dealt with, and conventions regarding signatures on documents, that, all of that, is done impeccably.

In fact recent French experience is very much marked by the impact of devolution of local accountabilities to local organizations and one key change was when responsibility for local town planning and *permis de construire* (planning permission) were delegated to local authorities. It rapidly became clear to the local councils that there would have to be changes in management approaches otherwise the costs of administering the system would become exorbitant and exceed the resources which had been devolved from central government. This in itself lead to a greater freeing up of approaches to financial and human resource management in French local authorities and served as a significant learning experience in how to manage the process of devolution.

David McGahey's view of the change in England is:

> You can't just say that you are going to do something and do it, even with those schools who are strongly committed to the LEA, you have to go out and win support and create partnerships. So the job of a senior Education

Officer is going to be a lot less desk bound, is going to spend a lot more time working with Headteachers, with Trade Unions and Professional Associations, with other organisations and agencies, and certainly much more corporately with other parts of the County Council and other aspects of government. So the job is much more about networking, about brokering, about fixing, about putting together deals of one sort or another than before. At the same time there has been much clearer focus on service delivery itself since over 80 per cent of the people working in Education Departments are actually delivering direct services either to the public or to schools. We have become much more aware of that fact and are having to work much harder ourselves to become customer friendly and responsive to customer needs. At a higher level we have had to get a lot more open and put ourselves around a lot more than we would have done a dozen years ago. We see it a lot more as the delivery of a service than the administering of a process than we did then.

The Political Dimension

All this change has meant a fundamental change in relationships at a local level. In France it has meant that the local elected politicians have some real authority on major issues, whereas before they would have been under the direction of the Prefect as the representative of the State. This in itself has represented a major change as Gilles du Chaffaut found when he joined the Pas de Calais Departement:

I was very struck, at the start when I arrived here, that there were a number of Councillors who asked me extremely deferentially if they could have a meeting with me. It was just the opposite of how I thought things should be. Of course it was all to do with how they had been used to operating with the Prefect, where, before decentralisation an elected councillor would have to go along on bended knee to some civil servant to see a file or whatever. Even the elected councillors hadn't really understood that they were in charge now and that the staff of the Département were there to follow their directions.

Similar changes took place in England, where, particularly in the shire counties the vast majority operated with hands-off politicians who attended formal committee meetings on a quarterly basis but who otherwise left the running of the authority to their full-time officers. This has changed drastically since 1980. According to David McGahey:

The other major difference, I think, is that the whole thing has got a lot more political with both a large and a small 'P'. With a small 'p' in the sense that you have to build networks of support for initiatives, but with a capital 'P' because Education is more centre stage both locally and nationally. So you have all the changes in Education and the fragmentation of the system in terms of the ownership of its various parts which has lead to a polarisation between local and central government with effectively those parts which have fragmented away being nationalised. All the arguments over resourcing have simply increased these tensions so the whole process has become much more politicised. So it is much more complex now and I don't think there is anybody who could survive at a senior level in a Local Education Authority these days without being a small 'p' political animal. This wouldn't have been the case a dozen years ago, where certainly in the shire counties in which I worked even Deputy Chief Education Officers wouldn't have had much to do on a day-to-day basis with the elected Members of the County Council, and probably not as much to do with Governing Bodies of schools and colleges either.

There are a number of effects from these changes in England and in France. The first is the impact externally where it is no longer clear who in this much more fragmented service delivery structure is responsible for what in the new order of things. This represents a loss of accountability and a much more complex way of working. In France Gilles du Chaffaut talks about a loss of 'lisibilite', of responsibility, to the community:

There is a complete loss of legibility in the system from the point of view of the citizen. It is not easy to work out what the state agencies do, and of course you can't work out what all the other the agencies are doing. There isn't a single document that tells you who is responsible for what, for example in relation to Colleges, High Schools and Universities. If you take the example of a University – is it the responsibility of the State, or the Regional Council or the Departement? There is an enormous loss of energy, for example, if you want to set up a project to counter the use of drugs and narcotics. Who do you have to go to for funding? You have to get everyone involved, the State, the Region, the *Département* and the Communes, you probably have to get the European level involved too. It's an enormous waste of effort, and when you see what is involved in setting up a cultural event it's worse because you have sponsors involved too!

Both managers argue that their roles have become far more 'political' than would have been the case before. In France this started from a fairly low base, since the local political groupings were relatively undeveloped.

The first election of a mayor of Paris based on universal suffrage took place in 1976 and the expansion in the role of the Council of the Départements (the Conseils Generals) dates only from 1982. Up to that time the elected local councillor was relatively subservient to the Prefect's office, which represented the French State at a local level and controlled all the major aspects of service delivery through an administrative bureaucracy.

In England the local political structure had been in existence for almost a century but had often been fairly passive, with councillors depending on the officer structure to run the local services. Financial constraints, forcing choices to be made between services, and the election of a more managerial breed of local councillors, many of whom believed that the way in which services were delivered (for example by outsourcing delivery to contractors) was as important as the service delivery itself, brought about rapid change, first in the big cities and latterly in the shire counties. In many cases local politicians took on active roles not dissimilar to that of the chairman of a private company, and many took a very hands-on approach to both the implementation of policy and the management of the organization. Dissatisfaction with some of the more extreme manifestations of this approach led to the establishment of the Widdicombe (1986) Committee and to the establishment of sets of rules on member involvement and of a monitoring officer in each local authority to ensure propriety and the avoidance of what were seen to be excesses in the use of politicians power of decision making.

In both countries, however, the result was the same. The emergence of an able and motivated political elite at local level galvanized the organizations which they controlled. As a result managers could no longer ignore the existence of politicians – to succeed they had to learn to work with them and to fulfil their agendas through an increasingly complex power-broking role with a range of other agencies.

The Managerial Environment

All this has led to a far more turbulent environment in which managers have to operate. More responsibility is passed down to operating units, management is a more complex activity and politicians are increasingly taking a hands-on approach and becoming actively involved in the day-to-day operations of public service organizations. This is often particularly disorientating for those who see themselves as professionals rather than

managers. Their perspectives are drawn from a particular body of knowledge and they often judge themselves against peer-defined standards. Some
have been powerful enough to resist many of the changes sponsored by
politicians. The police, for example, were able to ward off the bulk of the
proposals of the Sheehy report in the UK. Others have had to accommodate to new practices – although they have often achieved significant modi-
fication of the original proposals. Teachers in the UK, for example, managed
to achieve significant amendment to proposals for teacher appraisal by
gaining acceptance for their own agenda for the proposal (appraisal for
development rather than appraisal for judgement). These two experiences
of the changes on the two opposite sides of the Channel enable us to draw
some conclusions about the nature of management roles during the rest
of the decade.

The first is the importance of new skills and of management development in particular in managing in the more turbulent environment
presented by the 1990s. There can be no doubt that the nature of the management task has changed and the way managers manage is fundamentally
different. David McGahey describes it:

I probably spend a lot more time now than I did in the past on the telephone
and in meetings rather than sitting at my desk. I've no doubt that it's harder
work now than it was ten or twelve years ago. There is much more work to
be done in that much more complex environment and it is more time
consuming, more difficult, more sophisticated than it would have been in the
past. But that's not unattractive, there's no denying that it's a tougher but
much more interesting job than it was ten years or so ago. I'm sure you could
say the same thing if you were working in a Social Services environment or
in a Health Service Trust. All the changes over the past 10 years have
stimulated a more managerial culture, and that's a good thing.

Not surprisingly, the need to develop managerial skills in a very different way is recognized on both sides of the Channel. Whereas in the past
managers primarily needed knowledge of the system and of administrative
processes there is now a much broader agenda for management development in both countries. At one level this is concerned with individual skills.
Managers need to understand the system in which they operate, but they
also require a range of subtle influencing and social skills. This is reflected
in the recognition of 'competence-based' management development as a
way forward in the future in the UK which links to the system for National
Vocational Qualifications (NVQs). In France there is a highly developed

structure for training in the public sector through the work of the CNFPT (the National Centre for Internal Civil Service) which co-ordinates a range of training activities and influences best practice within local government organizations. The priorities within a *département* such as the Pas de Calais are:

> There are two things we have to get right internally. The first is human resources and that means proper recruitment and training and then the style of management, which is an area in which it is very important to continue improvements. In fact the improvement of management methods is still not being taken forward quickly enough whatever level of local government you are talking about in France.

The second major theme is the need to manage the discontinuity brought about by rapid changes in structural arrangements. This is summed up by the French phrase *'la perte de lisibilite'*. In France the solution was seen in very formal terms, about reorganizing services and opening local offices and service centres in centres of population. In England the response tended to be in 'softer' terms, concerned with becoming more customer friendly and relating to their needs. This was seen much more as a change of style rather than a change in the physical deployment of services on the ground.

This is communicated in a variety of ways. Both Kent County Council and the Pas de Calais Département have made great efforts to project a clear and positive corporate identity. The triangular logo of the Pas de Calais is to be seen in a range of locations and in the promotional publications of the *département*. Similarly in Kent there has been a clear and energetic approach to informing the populace of the role and functions of the County Council. A stylized rampant Kent horse is prominent on all county buildings and on the boundary points. The County Council has gone to great pains to explain its role in a series of leaflets and has commissioned the market research organization MORI to canvas residents on their views of the services provided by the County Council. It has been particularly noticeable how this has paid off during the recent local government review in England and Wales where there has been a strong local commitment to the retention of a strategic county-level role in Kent.

However, both our managers emphasized the importance of local integration of services. Again the French description of *'la polyvalence integrale de secteur'* is mirrored by David McGahey's description of:

a need for a coherent multi purpose framework. I can see some real advantages in a greater coherence between Education, Social Services, Health, Housing and Eonomic Development services at a local level. This is being recognized within institutions where they are saying that they need a framework which is broader than the institution and rather closer than Whitehall or a Regional Office in Reading or wherever.

So whatever the approach there can be little doubt that the issue of service coherence and integration at the local level is a key priority for both our managers and the organizations in which they operate.

This brings with it a range of new tensions. Bringing together disparate groups into multi-function organizations highlights the need to manage services across professional boundaries and develop an approach of multi-agency working. It also leads to the development of a cadre of general managers within the new organizations whose role transcends any one professional grouping. They may or may not be directly accountable to local politicians, however, as more and more 'arms-length' agencies are established. In particular, those charged with the management of such agencies need to recognize that they remain firmly within the public sector and that these services have not been privatized, nor are they in some way removed from the degree of accountability which applies to mainstream public service organizations.

In England the approach has been to peel off functions from democratic control in local government and to have them operate semi-autonomously with funding from national sources. In effect they have been removed from local political control and nationalized. The consequence of this has been to hamstring a significant part of the established functions of local authorities and to render them less capable of delivering some of the very programmes central government is pressing them to deliver. One example of this is the Government's desire to see the removal of surplus school places which inevitably leads to those schools short-listed for closure seeking survival through the grant maintained route.

In France the situation was very different. Traditionally there was a democratic dimension at local level in the communes, of which there are 35,000 in France ranging from the Commune of Paris, which has 35,000 employees to the smallest village with a budget of perhaps £4,000 a year, and which might only employ a part-time administrator, broadly similar to a parish council in England. At this level there were 500,000 elected councillors. In France there has also been a tradition whereby local politicians retain their local positions when they achieve higher office, so that Pierre Mauroy continued in his commune level position as Mayor of Lille when he was Prime Minister of France between 1981–3 as did his colleague Michel Delebarre who was both Mayor of Dunkirk and Minister of Transport. This pattern has been repeated at local level with elected councillors at the level of the commune (although normally those much smaller and less important than Lille or Dunkirk) retaining their positions at the level of the *département*. This leads to a whole range of challenges reflected in conflicting policies at the various levels and that current arrangements for grouping of local communes is based on indirect appointments to the higher-level institutions, many of which now find themselves handling very substantial multi-million-franc budgets.

So in France the problem is not the absence of a local democratic framework but the existence of one which is, if anything, excessive and over complicated, contributing to '*la perte de lisibilite*' of accountability for services. The French desire is for a much more positive approach to the amalgamation of commune-level authorities in order to achieve the economies of scale to enable the local framework to be built.

So while both our managers were experiencing a very similar pattern of change on the two sides of the Channel, both felt constrained by the absence of an effective local framework in which to operate. Furthermore, since both have been heavily involved in joint working wih their opposite numbers on the other side of the Channel, both have a perspective on the relative strengths of the other's situation. It is interesting that both envies the other in as far as the problems experienced in one country are more easily resolved in the other.

Gilles du Chaffaut sees the strength of other systems in their ability to restructure fundamentally their local government organization to meet the needs of changing times as the English did in 1974 and are now undertaking again through the work of the Local Government Commission. In France there is relative confidence in the ability of managers to improve the functioning of the organizations which have been created, but less certainty of the capacity to simplify the organizational complexity which has now been created.

English managers observe the process of devolution at work in France and the move from an administrative to a more managerial culture but with a very strong commitment to the development of democratically controlled local institutions and a very close working relationship between the central State and local authorities through well-developed 'contracts' and joint planning processes. They are struck by the leadership role which the chief executives of French organizations often take on, far more so than their English counterparts. Their perception is that, in France, there is a better chance of the right balance being struck between devolution and central control than is currently developing in English public services.

The French tradition is likely to mean that there will continue to be a strong link between national government and local institutions in France and that, as a result, it is unlikely that the market solutions now developing in England will ever be introduced into core public services in France. The strong local framework will continue to be a strength of French public services. Their managers will need to develop some of the softer personal skills which their English counterparts have acquired over the past decade.

English public services will, at the same time, have the strength of being run by managers with well-developed skills in the management of change and uncertainty. In time, as the need for effective relationships becomes recognized within both purchaser and provider organizations, it is likely that the voluntarist tradition in the UK will emerge in the shape of partnerships and voluntary planning arrangements.

At its core, though, there will be growing similarities between the roles which both English and French public service managers will be required to undertake and the competencies they will require to be successful. However the formal structures around them develop, this will place an increasing emphasis on the effective management of human resources in public services and the conscious and systematic development of those key management competencies.

Discussion Questions

1 Decentralization appears to be commonly seen as a way forward in the delivery of public services. What do you think the pros and cons of decentralization are?

2 What are the key differences between, and similarities with, the changing management role in the English and French system of local government?

3 Changes in the public service task require, it is argued, a move from administration to management. What are the implications of this?

Appendix 4.1: Description of the Systems

The Expansion of the Role of the *Département*

There have been two main features of French local government since the Revolution – the *département*, created in March 1790, and the prefect, a role created in 1798. The prefect had two roles:

- to act as the representative of the State within the *département*; and
- to exercise the executive authority of the *département*.

This system came to an end during the 1980s when the role of the prefect was redefined and the role of the *département* was enlarged. Various pieces of legislation in 1982, 1983 and 1985 have extended the traditional role of the *département* so that it now includes:

- Planning and transportation responsibilities;
- Social services roles (in respect of children, the handicapped and the elderly)
- Some education and leisure responsibilities;
- Economic development.

These involved a transfer of resources – both budgetary and staff, from the prefect to the *département*. As an example, in the Pas de Calais, which has a population of some 1.5m, around 1,800 social work staff transferred over to the *département*. It is fair to say that the allocation of financial resources to deliver the services has been an ongoing source of debate in France and in 1991 the Derosier Report, describing an *'incomplete decentralization'*, called for a further clarification of the roles of the various agencies.

The Diminution in the Role of the English County Council

Before 1988 the education system in England and Wales was essentially that of a national service, locally delivered. Most institutions and services were provided under the umbrella of the local education authority. This changed rapidly from 1988 onwards, largely but not exclusively through the effects of the 1988 Education Reform Act and the move towards local management in which extensive powers previously exercised by the LEA were delegated to the governors of individual schools and colleges and resource allocation was determined through formula funding processes.

The LEAs also lost major functions between 1988–94. These were:

- the polytechnics – which became self-governing in 1988;
- colleges of further education and sixth-form colleges – transferred to the Further Education Funding Council in 1993;
- under the Education Reform Act schools were able to 'opt out' of LEA control to become centrally funded; around 1,000 schools (60 in Kent) took this course of action.

5

Merging into Ribbon

MIKE DEMPSEY

Managing mergers is difficult enough for any manager. Few are likely to be in place with a body of experience which they can bring to bear on the complex processes involved. In trade unions the level of complexity involved in merging not only business structures and the staff within them but also democratic structures, activists and members is of a different order again.

This case study examines issues arising from a merger of three trade unions whom we shall call White, Purple and Green. It is particularly concerned with the cultural and human aspects of the process. Although the way some of the activities took place is trade-union specific, the management lessons are of much wider application. The framework used is that of A.F. Buono and J.C. Bowditch (1989), The human side of mergers and acquisitions. They suggest that there are seven stages in an organizational combination process (see table 5.1). This case study excludes the final two stages. The latter stage has not been reached and the aftermath stage may take some time.

This study is concerned primarily with the human and cultural aspects of the merger process but these, of course, are the most vital, if often the least attended to, aspects. The lessons, therefore, are of wide application despite the case being trade-union specific. They range over the way in which the various stages of the merger were managed, the effect of the cultural legacies of the old organizations, the way in which attempts can be made in a merger to create a new culture and how this can be done, the effect on performance and commitment and the particular problems created by the existence of a democratic structure in a not-for-profit organization. A final challenge is to form a view on how the final two stages could be

Table 5.1 The organizational combination process

Stage	Characteristics
1 Precombination	Degree of environmental uncertainty (technological, market, sociopolitical) may vary, but respective organizations are relatively stable, and members are relatively satisfied with the status quo
2 Combination planning	Environmental uncertainty increases, which preciptitates discussion concerning merger/takeover possibilities; fears arise that unless the firm grows larger companies will destroy it or the organization will become less competitive or even fail; the firm is still relatively stable, and discussion is confined to top executive level
3 Announced combination	Environmental uncertainty continues to increase, influencing decision; the organization is still relatively stable, and while members have mixed emotions concerning the merger, expectations are raised
4 Initial combination process	Organizational instability increases and is characterized by structural ambiguity (high) and some cultural and role ambiguity (low); although members are generally co-operative at beginning, goodwill quickly erodes
5 Formal physical–legal combination	Organizational instability increases as structural, cultural, and role ambiguities increase; mechanistic organizations take on some organic characteristics for a period; conflict between organizational members increases
6 Combination aftermath	High organizational instability, lack of co-operation, and 'we–they' mentality exist; violated expectations lead to intra- and inter-unit hostility; structural ambiguity decreases but cultural and role ambiguity remains high; dissenters leave the organization
7 Psychological combination	Organizational stability recurs as ambiguities are clarified, expectations are revised; renewed co-operation and intra- and inter-unit tolerance; time-consuming process.

Source: Reprinted with kind permission of Jossey-Bass Inc.

managed to achieve the goal of psychological combination. Can it, indeed, be achieved?

Pre-combination

Astrid Prolix, General Secretary of Ribbon, greeted the New Year with satisfaction but in deeply reflective mood. The past year had seen the merger of three long-established unions into one massive organization, of which she had become General-Secretary. She was proud of what had been achieved, but when she surveyed all the problems and the uncompleted strategies she felt she was entitled to allow herself the occasional doubt.

The three old unions had all been in the public sector but had widely different characteristics. White, the largest in terms of membership, staff and income, had represented white-collar staff at all levels in a range of services and industries. Astrid had been its General-Secretary. Purple, of a broadly comparable order of size in terms of members, though not of staff or income, had represented blue-collar workers in many of the same services and industries. Green, which joined the negotiations a year after they started, was a single-industry union representing a much smaller number of members in one major public-sector industry.

The merger sought to consolidate the position of the unions in the public sector and several privatized parts of it. There was, however, a strong vision driving the process – one of creating a completely new and modern organization giving 'a unified voice to the common interests of providers and users of services', representing 'a commitment to a social order embodying . . . caring values for all workers and the wider commu-nity' and in particular enabling the vast majority of women members of the new union to have an influence in the structures in proportion to their membership of it.

The three organizations had provided similar services to members in broadly the same employment sectors, though White provided far more services in-house. There were some independent units within the overall group, including a registered charity and travel and insurance companies. The intention was to seek economies of scale, but Astrid knew that unions had always been very bad at achieving such economies after merger. The merger was friendly in that it was consensually negotiated and approved by all stakeholder groups. These included members, activists and Executive Council members of all three organizations.

Environmental circumstances for merger were adverse. Trade union legislation had weakened unions. This included restrictions on rights to take forms of industrial action, and procedures which had to be followed in order to do so; expensive balloting requirements; and, in particular, a provision requiring unions to resign every three years every member who had their union subscriptions deducted from their salaries at source. Unemployment, contracting out of public services and the growth of individualist values leading, among other things, to the onset of unitarist, anti-union management styles, had all made the prospects for Ribbon less favourable than they appeared when it was conceived. If Astrid had not been an incurable optimist the prospects could have been very frightening indeed.

Combination Planning

Astrid reflected on the progress of the discussions between Purple and White.

Year 1

The discussions were the subject of a brief report to those unions' conferences. In that year Green joined the discussions as an equal partner, effectively restarting the process. As a smaller, sector-specific union, Green was concerned to secure a distinctive place for its traditions and values in any new organization. Astrid could see from the power of Ribbon's central industrial groups that it had succeeded.

Year 2

There was not much tangible progress but Astrid remembered with amusement the long, conceptual report which went to the three union conferences. She had joked with the friendly academic who had largely produced it that it had elevated platitudinization to a fine art. But, in retrospect, it had set the tone for the creation of a truly new organization with its own distinctive value systems. Out of it came the principle of 'member centredness' and the importance of semi-autonomous status within the structure for the various different public services, thus addressing Green's concerns. It also set the scene for the ideals of equal opportunities and fair representation (which were designed to advance the interests of women and prevent the domination of articulate, white-collar, staff). Many people felt these were vital; one of her new colleagues had expressed the view at the time that he deeply disliked Purple's culture which he described as 'macho and brutal – unless you happened to be one of the favourite sons'.

Year 3

Much more detail was included in the conference reports. In fact, by this time the level of detail probably exceeded that reached in most completed negotiations – but the members of White loved detail. Working parties had produced firm proposals on most aspects of the structure and organization of the new organization. Tremendous efforts had been made to produce proposals which were different from structures and practices of any of the three partners, even to the extent of finding new names for the new structures. One working party had called one part of the structure an aadvark and another an emu in order not to use words in discussion which reflected their own past experiences. The report had a mixed reception in White's conference, which carried many amendments.

Year 4

White had to hold a special conference in the spring to confront some of the problems this caused – not least the antagonism of Purple and Green to the behaviour of White's conference. This, though, was in some respects the turning-point and when the final report was presented to the three conferences that summer it was passed unamended in all of them.

Astrid felt that in one respect she had failed as chief executive during this period. Involvement of staff had been largely confined to senior managers and specialists. None of the three unions was accustomed to major change and many staff had probably felt that they would subsume their concerns in their immediate work. Some, certainly, did not believe it would ever happen; there was in one or two cases criticism of the concentration on the new union negotiations in management briefings. Yet in one particular respect, involvement and reassurance of the staff were even more important than in other merger processes. Trade union mergers have to be submitted to the members in a secret postal ballot. Without the staff working on all aspects of the campaign and ballot, the ballot could simply not be run.

The staff's trade unions had articulated many times the allegation that management had been prepared to put themselves out to work on all aspects of the merger except staff matters. Certainly, progress was slow. By the spring a staff protection agreement had been reached. This contained pledges that everyone who wanted a job in the new union could have one and there would be no compulsory redundancy – indeed, no member of staff would be required to move home. It also contained schemes for voluntary early retirement and voluntary severance. This was followed by a matching and slotting-in agreement in which the new organization was to come forward with management structures to which existing staff could be matched, singly or in competition. Rights of appeal against decisions made as part of this process were created, with an independent chair of an appeal committee.

The need for specification of detail, however, was as strong among the staff – particularly of White – as it was among the lay members who had attended the annual conferences. They also wanted things to stay very largely as they were. Astrid had tried to encourage them to see the positive things about interim and new structures as they were developed. 'Every new step into the new institutions', she told them, 'is a step into Ribbon. I understand that this may be uncomfortable and even painful but we are achieving a great enterprise together.'

Thus it was that the putative organization faced its first industrial dispute as White's trade unions told management that unless Ribbon's management structures were produced in two months staff would not work on the ballot. Management's response was that the demand was impossible to meet and that if it was maintained the whole enterprise would have to be abandoned. The resultant compromise was that White's managers would produce their submissions on what the new structures for their functions should look like. This was intended to be a participative process and result in a composite White view of the new union which would be presented to management consultants who had been appointed to prepare proposals on the new structures.

But this compromise was constructed in a spirit of confidence in the consultants, a firm headed by a former South African trade union leader who subsequently graduated and taught at Harvard Business School. After a series of interviews and hastily prepared reports the firm defaulted on its contract, which was terminated. Astrid was deeply bitter at how this had affected all her plans.

Announced Combination

Astrid was proud that, in year 4, there had been overwhelming votes in favour of the merger by the members of all three unions. White had the largest 'no' vote but it also had by far the highest poll.

Two consequences had flowed from the débâcle with management consultants. The first was a commitment to produce internal proposals for outline management structures by Christmas. Proposals dividing the new organization into three 'divisions', led by a deputy general-secretary, were devised and presented within that timescale. The objective was to make the first appointments, at regional level, as early in year 5 as possible and to take on other consultants to help to prepare the remaining structures before Vesting Day, 1 July.

The second was the taking over of a contract which the failed consultancy had had with an anthropologist who was undertaking a study of the cultures of the three organizations. She had presented a highly acerbic report early in year 5 and Astrid had had to work hard with her senior colleagues to help them to cope with some of the home truths it contained. A final report had been received later in the year. The first had been based on interviews with 240 staff and the second had supplemented those with interviews with key lay members.

Culture

The consultant had found that in White there was institutional inertia, in which discussion of problems was valued as an end in itself. A committee structure, similar to that contained in many public sector bodies but more labyrinthine, legitimized the work of managers and staff but was used as an excuse to duck and ignore problems and as a cover for not taking responsibility. She believed that institutional inertia had prevented the development of a strong management ethos.

In Purple it was the ability of management, without too much committee involvement, to make a fast and (what was believed to be) effective decision that was valued for its own sake. A greater degree of centralization had led to a belief that human and material resources were being used efficiently. But the lack of openness in taking those decisions meant that their rationale was all too often obscure. Consequently people were often left feeling resentful or manipulated by some alien authority.

In Green, she found, there was great value placed on informality but without any clear notion of accountability. The informality was a function of the smaller size of the organization and the single industry focus but the importance of informal networking left those who were not part of the network feeling as though they had to invent the organization for themselves. This was particularly noticeable in the gulf which existed between the agendas of head office and the regions.

Overall, she found differential valuation of staff with greater status afforded to those who might be seen to be 'solving world problems', mainly male, and those supporting them, mainly female. She pointed to the need to avoid the culture of the largest organization, White, dominating. She found that staff were looking for much more professional objective-setting, standards-based, styles of management which also met the aspirations of women staff. She therefore recommended systematic, in-house, programmes of management training which addressed these issues and used the experiences of staff at all levels to subvert accepted value systems.

Astrid had been heartened by the extent to which her senior colleagues had come on board in trying to tackle cultural issues. A colleague had recognized that 'the cultures of the three organizations are so different that we could end up in a cultural quagmire from which we will not be able to extricate ourselves because of the clash of cultures'. Another had commented that culture clash was a potential problem at all levels. 'The problem is on a continuum, being less of a problem with the membership, more with the activists and more still the greater that people are involved in the organization. In fact, the more people are at home in their old organizations, the more of a problem it will become.' Astrid's experience outside Ribbon had taught her that 'many of the cultures and sub-cultures will live on long after the old unions are part of history'.

Astrid was fortunate in having the odd tame Masters of Business Administration (MBA) student on the staff and one had done some research which also helped to illuminate this problem. It found that managers wanted to tackle the creation of Ribbon by building on the 'Aims and Values' which had been produced in the rule book – rather after the fashion of a mission statement. 'Aims and Values', one had said, 'will be seen as enhancing and empowering. They provide an accepted code; broad principles which say "this is why we're here". We must share them and measure their success.' Another had argued that they should be used 'not in the letter but in the spirit to manage diversity – a positive force, not a trip-wire. Staff should internalize the values so that one should not have to spell them out all the time'.

The recommendations of the research report reflected this, proposing an organization which was objective-centred, within which maximum autonomy would be devolved to managers and staff so that they would feel that they had a stake in creating Ribbon themselves. This autonomy would be devolved within a framework, including a budgetary framework, in which the respective roles of stakeholders – activists and full-time staff – would be explicitly defined. 'What we should be seeking is not autonomy from Ribbon but autonomy from bureaucratic clutter, in a partnership with elected members,' said a colleague. 'But I should prefer to have it being said that management and staff are doing too much than not doing anything at all.' Astrid knew, however, that 'in a democratic organization there

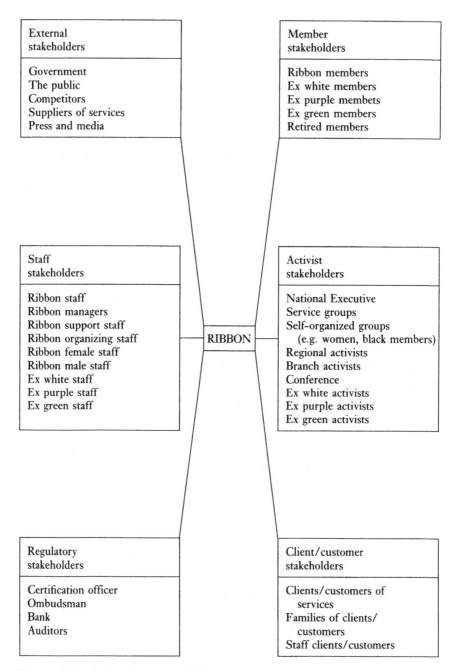

Figure 5.1 *Stakeholder map of Ribbon*

are limits to managerial control and influence. One can never operate in the same way as an employee of Shell or ICI'. The existence of a democratic structure had, of course, structural and management problems which, while they do not occur to the same extent in commercial mergers, would be common in the not-for-profit sector. They require a high level of stakeholder management capability. Some idea of the level required can be gleaned from figure 5.1, a stakeholder map of Ribbon.

The studies outlined above were inputs into the process of design and construction. The process, however, had been seriously delayed. Staff trade unions had refused to co-operate in the appointment of any staff at all in the regions until regional structures had been agreed. This did not take place until April and the first regional appointments took place in May. Senior managers had been slotted into the divisional structure earlier in the year (creating at least the perception that they had feathered their own nests) and the first managers at other levels of the structure were not appointed until July, with the intention that they would then devise structures for their new functions. Further, management had found it particularly difficult to communicate with staff. Never was communication needed more, but no system, and no staff, were in place to achieve this and the existing systems within the three old organizations were patchy.

Despite the luxury of a seven-and-a-half month gap between the ballot result and Vesting Day, therefore, and despite also the tremendous sense of achievement which Astrid and her colleagues had as Ribbon was born, ambiguity reigned on 1 July. The commencement of workshops throughout the country designed to train people to cope with change and ambiguity could never have been more opportune.

Initial combination

Astrid had been determined that Ribbon would be truly new. 'If we are agents of change, we must pioneer and we must challenge the old ways of doing things.' She had fought those who had tried to replicate their old structures and cultures, arguing that 'it is not possible to be caring and understanding in the new situation and then deny respect for others by hanging on to old practices'. She had got into trouble with some elected members by organizing activities enabling them to relate their roles to Ribbon's aims and values. She had also encouraged training programmes to enable herself and her managers to achieve their strategic objectives.

They had therefore planned workshops on management of change to involve, if possible, every member of staff (who also had access to the organization's employee assistance programme to enable advice and counselling to be available to them on a 24-hour basis). Courses for senior managers had been devised with a leading school of management. Astrid believed that training managers together was an important means of building the new organization and helping to create a climate in which a new culture could be forged. The courses themselves had at their core exercises which sought to identify the 'cultural webs' of the old organization and to devise a cultural web for the new one. Astrid was very proud of the vision her managers had shown in webs describing the nature of the organization the managers wanted to build and of the commitment to the building process they had demonstrated.

Astrid had insisted that the senior management team undertook training for its new role. 'Every time we involve ourselves in training which we would not have had in the old unions, we are taking steps into Ribbon,' said Astrid. 'We must also understand what we expect from each other so that we can exercise our managerial autonomy with confidence – but with accountability.' A workshop on team building was followed over a six-month period by two two-day sessions on strategic management skills.

One of the senior management team's first decisions had been to set up a project team to examine options for the acquisition of a new headquarters. Prior to merger there had been many conflicting views on how to approach the provision of services at national level. One objective had been to transfer resources closer to the members and therefore there was an assumption that national services would contract. There was also a feeling that many national functions were too large and might usefully be split up or spun out. But senior management took the strategic view that, if it proved economically viable, the best way of building the new organization with a new culture at national level was to get people first to become involved in the process of finding and equipping a new building and, second, to work together within it. 'The danger, however,' said a colleague, 'is that if members see a large headquarters building there will be a perception that central control is intended. And at the end of the day, it will be the members' decision, not ours.'

The setting up of a project team had been another important symbol of how the new organization was intended to work. The first, interim, management structures had been much more hierachical than was the ideal. But it had been felt that the way to achieve flatter, more co-operative ways of working was to encourage team- and project-based working. Workshops exploring the implications of this were organized and there was a proliferation of project teams which were expected to follow project management principles in which tasks were planned and achieved and the teams then disbanded – very different from White, where permament committees and working groups proliferated. Interestingly, one of Astrid's colleagues felt that this change did not necessarily mean more autonomy or responsibility for staff or management. 'Depending on how the senior management team operates,' he said, 'we could be substituting one set of constraints with another.'

But events had conspired to de-rail progress on the staffing front. Every stakeholder seemed to have different ends. The National Executive Committee (NEC) made it clear it wanted the reorganization to cost nothing. The staff unions were counting on salary drift in the assimilation of three salary structures into one. Staff themselves, retaining their old cultural expectations, anticipated new money for new jobs. Activists and members expected lower subscriptions as economies of scale were achieved. Management had totally failed to crack the nut of effective communication, and unofficial newsletters and spoof circulars began to appear. Astrid had had to issue a statement denying a rumour that all staff with less than two years service would have their contracts terminated. Individual managers had to deny that they were all being allocated luxury cars. 'If I feel like smiling, you'll all bloody smile,' said Astrid, trying to enliven one particularly difficult and depressed management meeting.

Astrid had been depressed at the demoralization and reduction in performance which occurred, together with idealization of the past which was part of it. One of White's characteristics had been a more adversarial industrial relations structure and tradition, and it was not surprising therefore that this began to manifest itself as staff, a large majority of whom were formerly employed by White, became more unsettled.

Formal Combination

The publication of proposed staffing structures had not led to the relief that senior management expected. Although staff had guarantees about their future, they found many of the relativities and relationships difficult to accept and they believed that staff of the other were doing better than them. People were not being allowed voluntary severance until new structures were adopted and it could be guaranteed that they would not be replaced.

Yet Astrid was determined to maintain her strategic focus. She encouraged her organization development unit to develop the management of change and the building of the new organization. 'It needs to think laterally and forward and be able to see round corners.' She wanted to develop a participative management style and communicate properly. 'We need to develop a climate of openness in decision making, to bring people with us.' She insisted on a strategic training and development policy and on a budget to match. She knew that she and all her senior colleagues needed continuing training. 'None of us has been trained in this task,' she said. 'We know what we want but we have inadequate training and experience to achieve it.'

She was also determined to rationalize headquarters functions in a new building. The strong opposition to it which was gathering, she felt, was culturally based because failure to move to a new building would result in the most powerful cultural symbol of them all, one of the old union's buildings becoming the headquarters of Ribbon. But she, too, was concerned to ensure than a new headquarters would not mean greater central control. The senior management team wanted headquarters to be a resource, not a controlling force, but several of her colleagues were alarmed at the significant power base of the industrial groups at national level. 'Instead of ending up with strong central departments or regional baronies, we could find the industrial groups being the pivotal forces,' said one. 'Undue power at any level would not be a happy outcome. Everyone has to have their share of the action.'

The story of building the new organization was, then, far from complete. As Astrid contemplated the New Year, she felt, as she often did, almost overwhelmed by the enormity of the project at the same time as she felt pride at what had so far been achieved. 'The real challenge', she thought, 'is change itself. Unions have by and large been unsuccessful in meeting change. We will not follow their example.'

Discussion Questions

1　Why did existing cultures make merger problematic?

2　What was the implementation strategy adopted by Ribbon?

3　Is it likely that Ribbon will reach stage 7 in the Buono and Bowditch schema?

Reference

A.F. Buono and J.C. Bowditch, *The human side of mergers and acquisitions*, San Francisco, CA: Jossey-Bass, 1989.

6

The Metropolitan Police Plus Programme*

GARRY ELLIOTT

As Sir Peter Imbert, the Commissioner of the Metropolitan Police (the Met), prepared to hand over to his successor in 1993, problems surrounding the policing of London appeared to be as great as ever. Calls for greater accountability and value for money were strong. The view of many of those involved in police funding or competing with the police for a share of the public sector funds could be summed up in the tone of an earlier editorial in *The Times*: 'For the Police Federation yesterday to accuse the Government of undervaluing its work is little short of cheek. No group in the public sector has been more succoured by Home Secretaries since Mrs Thatcher came to power in 1979. Certainly no group has been treated so well with so little obvious return' (*The Times*, 23 May 1990).

Early rumours about the findings of an enquiry into police pay and conditions chaired by the industrialist Sir Patrick Sheehy were affecting morale, and amalgamations of forces and changes in methods of funding and control were expected in a Government White Paper soon to be published. On top of this some *cause célèbres* and highly publicized allegations of police malpractice were still fresh in people's minds and affecting public confidence in the police service generally. The next five years looked as full of interest, change and problems as the previous five.

As Sir Peter prepared for his retirement he was asked which of his achievements as Commissioner he would put first. He replied, 'Well, I

* The case was made possible by the generous assistance of the Metropolitan Police Service.

haven't really achieved it yet. I intended the Plus Programme to change the Met from a force to a service, not only in the eyes of the serving officers, but more importantly in the minds of the public' (*The Job*, January 1993).

The PLUS Programme, a project to change the culture of the Met, had been ambitious. It had started in 1987 when, as one of his first actions at being appointed, Sir Peter commissioned a team of consultants to look at the corporate identity of the Met in response to a perception of falling public confidence and a belief that internal problems and divisions were hampering the effectiveness of the force (see Background Note 'The Metropolitan Police' pp. 114–117).

This case examines how a public service seeks to change its culture in the light of competing objectives and perceptions of its function.

The Environment

The Metropolitan Police was unique among British police forces in that the Home Secretary acted as the police authority charged with ensuring that the force was properly resourced and efficiently managed, a function that for forces outside London was performed by a committee of elected councillors and magistrates. It was a matter of dispute by some groups whether the needs of Londoners would be better served by their own elected police authority. One of these groups which was quite vociferous was the Police Monitoring and Research Group of the London Strategy Policy Unit which had been set up by nine London boroughs to carry through the policy initiatives of the disbanded Greater London Council. In the conclusion to the report on the Metropolitan Police financial estimates for 1987–8 they wrote:

> Public dissatisfaction with the organisation and management of the Met's finances is growing. Primarily this is caused by a lack of commitment within the force to provide value for money services. This year's estimates contain ample proof of the waste in resources caused by a poor structure of exercising management controls. This has been picked up by the House of Commons Public Accounts Select Committee which, although not in a position to propose that control of the police service should transfer from the Home Secretary, was evidently very unhappy about the way financial matters and policy co-ordination has failed (Police Committee Support Unit, London: Greater London Council, February 1986).

The financial environment for the Met was changing. In common with all public sector organizations it had been cash limited for the past three years and although it had enjoyed increases in its funding it was having to come to terms with a tightening on budgetary control. The funds came from two main sources: about half the net expenditure of the force was met from local authority rates and the remainder by way of government grants. See Appendix 6.3 for a summary of the functional cost information.

The world for the police was also changing in other ways. Responsibility for the prosecution of offenders had been taken away from the police in the previous year with the creation of the Crown Prosecution Service and officers were still coming to terms with their altered role.

Cause célèbres of police wrongdoing surrounding some high-profile court cases had been guaranteed to reach the front pages of national newspapers and had appeared to dent the support and confidence of the vast majority of the public which the Met had enjoyed. A survey in 1988 found that 69 per cent of Londoners polled thought that the police were doing a very or fairly good job (Appendix 6.4). Whether this was itself a good or bad message for the organization was less important than the fact that the figure was showing a distinct downward trend and this was a cause for concern especially as the survey went on to suggest that people in non-White ethnic groups were less likely to have a high opinion of the work done by the police.

Coupled with this the British Crime Survey suggested that nationally crime had increased by 30 per cent in the past six years and that only 37 per cent of crime was reported to police. Reported crime was increasing sharply in London and the proportion of crimes cleared-up by police was not keeping pace (Figure 6.1).

The surveys commissioned annually by the Met were part of a broad process of consultation whereby the force determined the views of the people in London. Despite minor variations, the results of these had shown a consistency over several years (Appendix 6.5).

At a local level consultative committees had been set up on all London boroughs as a result of the 1986 Police and Criminal Evidence Act. These were innovations which followed the recommendations of Lord Scarman in his report following the riots in Brixton several years previously. Consultative groups were committees of councillors and other local people and it gave them the opportunity to meet and question the chief superintendent in charge of policing their area. As a group they had no executive power but were a vehicle for consultation and communication.

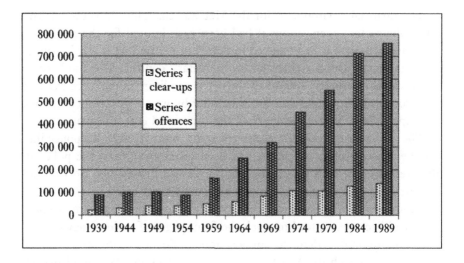

Figure 6.1 *Offences and clear-ups in the Metropolitan Police Division –*
1939–1989
Source: Annual Report of the Commissioner of the Metropolitan Police, London, 1988.

The Birth of the Plus Programme

In September 1988 the consultants commissioned by Sir Peter published
their report, 'A Force for Change' and, while pointing to great strengths
within the Met, it made suggestions in several areas, the principal one
being their perception that the Met lacked a common sense of purpose.
They commented:

> There is no consistency of views on the overall mission of the Met, nor how
> each individual contributes to the whole. Police work is based on the prin-
> ciple that individual police officers are given a high degree of independence
> of action and discretion. This means that each police officer interprets polic-
> ing in the way he thinks best (Metropolitan Police Service, 'A Force for
> Change', 1989).

They also highlighted other matters which exacerbated this, such as internal divisions between police and civil staff or even between officers
performing different roles. They felt that presentation and channels' of
communication should be improved and the role and structure of management should be reviewed in the light of the changing environment in which
the Met was working. The report also pointed to the strengths of the Met,

the renowned centres of excellence and the willingness to face change, but it gave Sir Peter significant cause for thought and concern.

The Commissioner tasked DAC Charles Pollard to take the report and turn the recommendations into an action plan. At the same time he considered further the idea of a mission statement which would be relevant to all the Met's personnel and act as a focus and vehicle for the change he knew was necessary.

The Metropolitan Police had always had a statement of its primary objects which was credited to Richard Mayne and was still learned word perfect by every constable when they did their initial training:

> The primary object of an efficient police is the prevention of crime. The next that of detection and punishment of offenders if crime is committed. To these ends all the efforts of police must be directed. The absence of crime, and the maintenance of public tranquillity will alone prove whether these efforts have been successful.

How relevant was this to the late twentieth century? Traditionally, police mission statements were concerned with:

- upholding the law and guarding the peace;
- preventing crime;
- detecting criminals and bringing them to justice;
- helping the public.

Much of police work has a social services/education flavour to it such as assisting people who are locked out of their homes or working with school children. Previous research into modern police work had shown that the majority of calls from the public were not crime related and incidents such as domestic occurrences, road accidents, lost and found property, missing person cases, errands, health- and animal-related matters accounted to 59 per cent of all incidents.

Sir Peter had already started the debate on this subject around the service and he used a conference in October 1988 to discuss and develop these ideas with his senior staff. A need to keep any statement short and simple was recognized and there was a general dislike for the term 'mission statement', the preference being for a 'statement of purpose'. A draft was produced – 'The purpose of the Metropolitan Police is "To serve and Protect" '. The draft went on to list ten values of every member of the organization including adopting 'the highest standards', upholding 'individual rights', being neither 'racist nor sexist' and being 'cost effective'. This was circulated in the organization, inviting comment.

'Making it Happen'

In April 1989, DAC Pollard's report 'Making it Happen' was published which recommended work under nine components and launched the Statement of Common Purpose and Values of the Metropolitan Police Service.

Statement of our Common Purpose and Values

> The purpose of the Metropolitan Police Service is to uphold the law fairly and firmly; to prevent crime; to pursue and bring to justice those who break the law; to keep the Queen's Peace; to protect, help and reassure people in London; and to be seen to do all this with integrity, common sense and sound judgement.
>
> We must be compassionate, courteous and patient, acting without fear or favour or prejudice to the rights of others. We will need to be professional, calm and restrained in the face of violence and apply only that force which is necessary to accomplish our lawful duty.
>
> We must strive to reduce the fears of the public and so far as we can, to reflect their priorities in the action we take. We must respond to well founded criticism with a willingness to change.

The project taking forward this report was called 'Plus' and a team was set up with separate groups looking at each of the nine components. When launching the project, Sir Peter said that it was 'one of the most important steps we as an organization are to take over the next few years' (*The Job*, 14 April 1989). He added that he was determined that the bulk of the programme of change would be carried out during his term of office. The Plus programme is best described as an attempt to change philosophy and culture rather than a specific set of tangible reforms.

The components of the programme were:

1   adopting the Statement of our Common Purpose and Values;
2   policy making and command systems;
3   composition of front-line teams;
4   deployment of front-line teams;
5   rewards and sanctions;
6   communication;

7   paperwork and bureaucracy;
8   appearance of the force;
9   performance indicators.

Sir Peter realized that action in all these areas was necessary if his ideas for the service were going to come to fruition. Teams were set up under the control of a specially selected commander to pursue each component individually. John Smith, the Assistant Commissioner in charge of Management Support, was appointed as project manager and at the launch he gave his view of a rationale behind the ideas: 'We are putting the emphasis on service to the public, forging relationships with the community. This is not a softly, softly approach. Every good detective knows for example that he can obtain more information if people are treated well. Our contract with the public will mean that we learn more about crime' (*The Job*, 14 April 1989).

Despite the breadth of the Plus programme, two items lay at its heart: the adoption of the Statement of Common Purpose and Values and the senior policy-making structure. It was important that action on these had top priority.

The Implementation of Common Purpose and Values

Sir Peter was always aware that the statement would need action to support it if it was to be accepted and be of value. He knew that it would need to overcome some resistance if it was to become part of the core values of the service. The issue of the Metropolitan Police Service (MPS) internal newspaper, *The Job*, following the launch carried a letter to the editor which stated, 'The expression of our Purpose and Values for the 1990s seems little different to those pertaining in the 1890s or the 1830s. It is perfectly acceptable as a statement of intent although I thought that it was already part and parcel of everyday police work' (*The Job*, 28 April 1989).

Although wide consultation had been carried out prior to the statement being decided, it was new to most of the service and it was important that it was discussed and reinforced. Framed copies were distributed and very soon were displayed in all MPS buildings and most offices. The Component 1 Team then set to work on how ownership could be achieved since values statements are never absorbed by being pinned to a wall.

In the winter and spring of 1990 four seminars for 600 of the most senior police and civil staff in the organization were arranged at the training school at Hendon. These were designed to introduce the most senior management to the plans and processes being prepared and to set the scene for day-long seminars which were being arranged for all staff which were planned to start in June.

During the summer the Commissioner addressed large groups of his middle management at specially prepared presentations at the Westminster Theatre. The sessions were designed to ensure that the managers on the divisions and in the branches at headquarters understood the change that was taking place and played their part in selling it throughout the organization. Sir Peter summed it up:

> PLUS will make us a more effective organisation. How will it do that? By giving us a sense of unity, a common purpose. By improving leadership across the organisation. By giving us a positive attitude to the concept of service both between ourselves and in our dealings with the public. By making us less defensive and isolated. By improving the way we communicate both within the organisation and outside. All this amounts to profound cultural change . . .

The magnitude of this task of putting all 44,000 members of staff through the seminars was not underestimated and careful plans were prepared to ensure that the days involved a mixture of ranks, roles and lengths of service. A video explaining the issues and featuring the Commissioner was produced which would be used to start and end each day. Glossy briefing packs were prepared for each attendee and a process to ensure that they were briefed before and debriefed after the day by their line managers was arranged.

The seminars started on 3 September 1990 under the title 'Working together for a better service', and a year later 99 per cent of the workforce had been through the process. Not all the reaction was positive. The facilitators had to deal with a full range of views and feeling about the programme. Some officers who felt that they were already giving a good service felt hurt. In the feedback from one of the sessions a detective constable said: 'Some senior officers fail to understand the problems affecting constables and sergeants and the officers react somewhat unfavourably towards the statement [of purpose] when rammed down their throats by such officers.'

It is a difficult task to restore a sense of corporate identity when relationships between senior and junior officers are strained. Authoritarian management breeds cycicism and mistrust. Others saw the programme as being too much like a business, taking away from the principle of public service.

A uniform constable commented: 'In general the Plus programme is ideal – however the seminar on the day reminded me of working in industry again. I can't see how we can compare the service to outside industry.'

The Operational Policing Review

At the same time as the Plus team were struggling with the difficult issues and the seminars were being held, a major review sponsored jointly by the ACPO, the Superintendents Association and the Police Federation was published. It was a lengthy document covering all aspects of the service and among its headlines it pointed to an erosion in the level of 'traditional' policing and felt that the drive towards efficiency had reduced the sense of service.

Surveys had been carried out to gain the views of members of the public, members of consultative groups and police officers. While there was broad agreement in some areas, e.g. the priority of the police in dealing with emergencies, it was evident that there was a mismatch between the attitude of the public and the police and not a clear agreement between the public and members of consultative groups.

There was a strong consensus among members of the public that more police should be patrolling on foot and more than 80 per cent said that, of the police officers they saw, too many were in vehicles. The great majority saw preventing crime as a particularly important police activity and many more people said that they preferred the caring, community style of police officer to the firm, law enforcement style (Appendix 6.6).

Although public opinion strongly favours uniformed patrol, there appears to be little evidence that, as a deterrent to crime, it is that effective. The PC on the beat passes within 100 yards of a burglary in progress once every eight years. However, the physical presence of the police is seen as reassuring.

In comparison, police officers responding conversely placed relatively low importance on the community constable type role and did not see an increase in foot patrols as desirable.

The Home Secretary may take a different view of the role of the police. The government identified a number of priorities for 1994 in order to reduce violent crime and increase the number of detected burglaries. These priorities were crime fighting, upholding the law, bringing criminals to justice and providing value for money. ACPO has sought to identify other priorities. They involve community relations, public reassurance and the maintenance of order. ACPO recognize that much of police work is not directly involved with catching criminals and that the development of good police–community relations is of paramount importance to them.

The Policy-making and Command Structure

Soon after the launch of the Plus programme a consultant was commissioned to work with a small team of a chief superintendent and a senior civil staff member to pursue component 2 and look at the senior policy-making structure of the Met. Six years previously an annual planning cycle based loosely on management by objectives had been introduced where divisions set their own objectives in the light of published force goals. These were monitored and co-ordinated by units on each area and by the Force Planning Unit at New Scotland Yard who was responsible to the Commissioner for preparing strategic reports to the Home Secretary.

Separate to this, resources were bid for through a process governed by the Government Public Expenditure Survey (PES) cycle. Bids were aggregated and prioritized by areas. The Receiver was then responsible for preparing the submission to the Home Office for resources that would be needed in the financial year two years following the bid.

The team reported in 1990, highlighting a need for:

- the Metropolitan Police to take a longer forward view and consider a five-year strategy;
- the Policy Committee to delegate as much as feasible and concentrate on the most important decisions affecting the service including the strategic review;
- operational and resource planning to be aligned.

They suggested a structure where operational policy could be delegated to ACTO and ACSO, and support issues to the Receiver, and at the same time ensuring users and providers of resources were both involved in decision making. Three new committees ('Executives') were recommended:

1   the Territorial Operations Executive (TOE), chaired by ACTO and involving not only all DACs but the directors of the departments under the control of the Receiver;
2   the Specialist Operations Executive (SOE), chaired by ACSO and with a similar membership to the TOE but considering operational issues falling to SO Department;

3   the Support Executive, chaired by the Receiver and involving the directors of his departments and also the assistant commissioners 'MS' and 'PT' and the DACs 'TO' and 'SO'.

The new structure was set up at the end of 1991 and in November the first five-year plan was presented to the Home Office as the Police Authority, setting out the 'Strategic Intention' and containing manpower and budget proposals for the years 1993–7. The Strategic Intention had seven principal strands:

1   To remain a visible, predominantly unarmed, approachable police service in order to provide a reassuring presence across London. This, our overriding policing style, has its roots deep in the community.
2   To increase consultation with the public and their representatives; to inform and to respond to their views, and their particular and changing needs, as far as we can; and to improve our internal communications. We intend to maintain our place as leaders in policing philosophy and practice.
3   To establish a clear view of the relative importance of policing tasks, and improve our performance in those areas of police activity which are identified for priority attention. It may be necessary deliberately to divert manpower away from some areas of work to address these priorities.
4   To maintain a range of specialist services which, in support of our general policing style, reflect the changing and dynamic needs of those living and working in London. Such specialisms must also encompass those national responsibilities we presently bear.
5   To achieve a sufficiency and disposition of personnel – both police and civilian support staff – to make us more effective in the delivery of our service and to realize the full potential of all individuals within the service promoting professionalism together with high standards of personal conduct. All personnel must be well trained, led and managed.
6   To ensure technical and other appropriate support for our workforce. Investment here must be sustained and have as its twin goals the greater effectiveness of staff and the provision of better working conditions for them;
7   Finally, to give a high quality service to all our customers, particularly the public, delivered in a way that represents good value for money. This requires exacting self-scrutiny of our performance, against agreed standards, through inspection and review procedures. We will continue

to promote good practice and correct errors; if we are wrong and
grievances are justified, we will accept our mistakes.

Discussion Questions

1 How well has the Met responded to the interests of its key
  stakeholders?

2 Has the Met been successful in moving from a police force to a
  police service?

3 What lessons can be learned concerning changes in public services
  culture?

Background Note: the Metropolitan Police

The force which Sir Peter had taken over was very similar to that which
he had joined as a constable 34 years previously and in some ways it had
not changed in over 100 years. Primacy was still given to the idea of the
unarmed uniformed constable patrolling on foot supervised by a structure
similar to the army one on which it was based. Written reports were often
passed through several layers of hierarchy before achieving their object.
CID officers (or detectives) working in plain clothes investigated crimes
which had been reported.

The Met had about 28,000 police officers supported by 16,000 civil staff.
Apart from patrolling in uniform and investigating crime the police officers'
roles varied between traffic policing, dealing with accidents, illnesses and
deaths, and managing demonstrations. In a *Guide to the Met* published in
1986 the Greater London Council had attempted to list the range of police
duties and had suggested that some of them were controversial and could
be done by local authorities. The list was:

- crime prevention;
- crime detection;
- assisting people (e.g. providing information, lost property);
- social services (e.g. children in care, missing persons);
- traffic control;
- public order, e.g.
  - day to day control of streets,
  - control of large crowds (e.g. football crowds, demonstrations),

- dealing with public disorder,
- policing industrial disputes;
• national functions (e.g. royalty and diplomatic protection);
• political and industrial surveillance (work of special branch);
• public and community relations.

The hierarchy of ranks of police officers is shown at Appendix 6.1 Legislation prevented officers from being part of a trade union, but three staff associations existed to represent members at a local and national level. The Association of Chief Police Officers (ACPO) represented the most senior, and through a series of committees acted as means of making and co-ordinated national policy. The superintendents' association similarly represented superintendents and chief superintendents and the Police Federation acted for constables to chief inspectors.

Civil staff roles included traffic wardens, scenes of crime examiners and photographers, engineers, surveyors, drivers and administration work. The grade structure broadly followed civil service lines. Programmes to civilianize jobs which were felt not to require the skills, training, experience or powers of a police officer had been an important part of efficiency measures for a number of years. Civil staff were represented through several trade unions which recognized the range of civil staff roles covering both industrial and non-industrial work.

Police and civil staff had separate career structures and usually separate lines of reporting. All promotion for police was from within the service. All senior officers for a number of years had once walked the streets as constables.

The structure of the organization had been radically changed three years previously (Figure 6.2) and the force was now split into eight geographical areas, one covering the central area and the rest dividing London like slices of cake. Each area was under the control of a deputy assistant commissioner (DAC). Each DAC was responsible for the work of about nine police divisions together with units attached to the area headquarters such as traffic enforcement and a mobile reserve. A policing division was an area usually covered from a single station but containing more than one station in the larger divisions towards the edge of London. A division was headed by a chief superintendent.

The force headquarters centred around a tower block in Central London where Sir Peter had his office on the eighth floor. Known throughout the world as New Scotland Yard it carried on the name of the site of the first

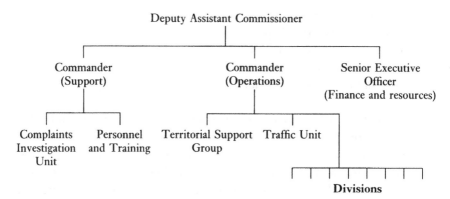

Figure 6.2 *Metropolitan Police area structure*

Metropolitan Police headquarters over 150 years previously. Management of the Metropolitan Police was actually shared between Sir Peter, who as Commissioner was the operational head, and the Receiver, a senior civil servant responsible for finance and resources. This division of responsibility had been the case since 1829 when the Metropolitan Police had been set up with joint Commissioners Charles Rowan and Richard Mayne and a Receiver 'to administer all monies applicable to the [Police] Act'.

The headquarters was divided into 11 departments, four under the control of assistant commissioners and seven under the Receiver. Appendix 6.2 shows the structure of headquarters and the responsibilities of the departments. The police departments were:

1 *Territorial Operations* – responsible for all police functions on divisions and areas and central functions such as public order and obscene publications.
2 *Specialist Operations* – responsible for all crime not capable of being dealt with on a local basis including terrorism, fraud, robbery and international crime. Also provides national functions such as protection of the Royal Family and diplomats.
3 *Management Support* – responsible for enhancing management practice, planning and policy.
4 *Personnel and Training* – responsible for recruiting, career development and training of police officers.

The senior decision-making group was called the Policy Committee and met fortnightly, chaired by the Commissioner. It comprised the Deputy Commissioner, the four Assistant Commissioners, the Receiver and the Deputy Receiver. Meetings were often preceded by a co-ordinating committee attended only by the police officer members where operational matters were discussed.

The police force that Sir Peter inherited when he joined the Met was not dissimilar in culture and structure to police forces elsewhere. Police forces were traditionally hierarchical, centralized and authoritarian and with strict adherence to a rigid set of rules. As police forces increasingly split into specialized divisions the development of a coherent and integrated service delivery could be hindered by the divisions between central headquarters and operational elements.

In common with many other parts of the public services, the police force was slow to recognize the importance of meeting public expectations and tended to be producer-driven.

Appendix 6.1: Ranks of Police Officers in the Metropolitan Police

Commissioner

Assistant Commissioner

Deputy Assistant Commissioner

Commander

Chief Superintendent

Superintendent

Chief Inspector

Inspector

Sergeant

Constable

The ranks constable to chief superintendent have equivalent 'detective' ranks for officers working in the CID

Appendix 6.2: Senior Management Structure of the Metropolitan Police in 1989

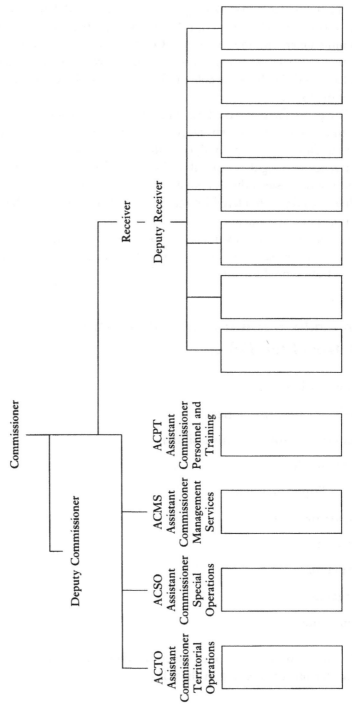

Figure 6.3 *Senior management structure of the Metropolitan Police in 1989*

Appendix 6.3: Metropolitan Police

Table 6.1 Summary of functional cost information

	Annual cost £K of function	% of gross force budget
Patrol	341,805	28
CID	155,271	13
Uniform officers in crime squads	50,945	4
Traffic	74,968	6
Community relations	16,532	1
Public order	25,507	2
Training	53,357	4
Complaints and discipline	9,743	1
Protection duty	41,357	3
Police: Other HQ functions	29,557	3
Other Area and divisional duties	236,054	20
Civil staff: Other HQ functions	110,569	9
Other Area and divisional duties	22,024	2
Civil staff overtime	19,064	2
	1,186,753	98

The remaining 2 per cent reflects expenditure which cannot be usefully apportioned to individual functions.

Adapted from the *Annual Report of the Commissioner for the Metropolis*, 1988.

Appendix 6.4: Perception of Police Performance 1983–1989

Table 6.2 'Taking everything into account, would you say that the police in this area do a good job or a poor job?'

	1983 %	1984 %	1985 %	1986 %	1987 %	1988 %	1989 %
Very good	25	25	22	18	18	18	16
Fairly good	47	48	47	48	49	51	48
Combined positive image	72	73	69	66	67	69	64
Neither	10	9	10	11	12	11	14
Fairly poor	6	6	7	8	7	7	8
Very poor	2	3	3	4	4	4	4
Combined -ve image	8	9	10	12	11	11	12
Uncertain	10	9	10	12	10	10	11

From annual public attitude surveys commissioned by the Metropolitan Police Service.

GARRY ELLIOT

Appendix 6.5: Personal Safety and Policing Priorities 1983–1989; Safeguarding Property 1986–1989

Table 6.3 'How safe do you feel walking alone in this area after dark?'

	1983 %	1984 . %	1985 %	1986 %	1987 %	1988 %	1989 %
Very unsafe/unsafe	48	51	56	48	48	50	47
Women only	65	72	74	70	66	70	67
Reasons							
Fear of mugging	62	43	52	43	30	32	28
General fear	12	31	31	29	26	29	29

From annual public attitude surveys commissioned by the Metropolitan Police Service.

Table 6.4 'What do you feel are the most important problems in this area that the police should concentrate their efforts on?'

Rank order Offence	1983 %	1984 %	1985 %	1986 %	1987 %	1988 %	1989 %
1 Burglary	38	39	35	39	38	31	34
2 Mugging	27	22	24	19	26	24	20
3 Vandalism	15	15	13	14	14	13	14
4 Traffic	10	6	6	7	8	8	11
5 Loitering	8	6	8	9	9	9	9

Subjects were asked to place 18 categories in order of priority. The chart shows the top five categories and the percentage of people giving that category the highest priority. From annual public attitude surveys commissioned by the Metropolitan Police Service.

Table 6.5 'In what ways, if any, do you think that the police could help the public safeguard their own property from theft?'

	1986 %	1987 %	1988 %	1989 %
More police on foot	38	50	50	51
Encourage Neighbourhood Watch Schemes	22	24	27	28
More police patrols	12	20	20	23
Information/leaflets	19	13	12	15
Visits from Crime Prevention Officers	15	13	10	13
Property marking	3	4	5	6
Advertising	7	3	3	3

From annual public attitude surveys commissioned by the Metropolitan Police Service.

Appendix 6.6: Policing Priorities

There is a high level of agreement about the order of policing priorities.

Table 6.6   Policing priorities – Tasks

	Rankings	
	Public	Police
Respond immediately to emergencies	1	1
Detect and arrest offenders	2	2
Investigate crime	3	3
Patrol the area on foot	4	5
Set up squads for serious crime	5	7
Provide help and support to victims of crime	6	9
Get to know local people	7	4
Give advice to the public on how to prevent crime	8	8
Patrol the area in cars	9	6
Work closely with local schools	10	10
Work with local council departments, such as housing, to plan crime prevention	11	12
Control and supervise road traffic	12	11

Source: Operational Policing Review, Joint Consultative Committee, 1990, quoted in Audit Commission, undated.

The consensus begins to break down over the offences which the police should devote most time to fighting.

Table 6.7   Policing Priorities – offences

	Rankings	
	Public	Police
Sexual assaults on women	1	3
Burglary of people's houses	2	1
Drunken driving	3	8
Vandalism and deliberate damage to property	4	9
Robberies in the street involving violence	5	2
Crimes in which firearms are used	6	4
Use of heroin and other hard drugs	7	5
Theft of and from motor cars	8	7
Fighting and rowdyism in the streets	9	6
Litter and rubbish lying around	10	14
Use of cannabis/pot/marijuana	11	13
Parking and general traffic offences	12	12
Bag-snatching and pick-pocketing	13	10
Racial attacks	14	11
Noisy parties and domestic disturbances	15	15

Source: Operational Policing Review, Joint Consultative Committee, 1990.

References

Annual Report of the Commissioner of the Metropolitan Police, 1988.
The Job, 14 April 1989.
The Job, 28 April 1989.
The Job, January 1993.
Metropolitan Police Service, 'A Force for Change', 1989.
Police Committee Support Unit, *Guide to the Met*, London: Greater London Council, February 1986.
The Times, 23 May 1990.

7

Implementing Community Care

ALAN LAWTON

Formulating policies is a key element in the strategic process. However, attending to the implementation of those policies is also crucial. Implementation is a crucial part of strategy. This case is concerned with issues of implementation. As such it is concerned with a number of key themes:

- the suitability and feasibility of policy proposals from the perspective of financial and human resources;
- the acceptability of policy proposals to the affected stakeholders including politicians, managers and service users;
- the challenges of implementing policies that require the co-ordination of different professionals and organizations;
- solving the operational problems;
- the relationship between strategy formulation and implementation.

The case focuses upon the implementation of care in the community in a fictional local authority. The Background Note (pp. 135–40) gives information concerning care in the community and illustrates some of the issues that it has generated.

Stourvale and Community Care

Stourvale was a traditional multi-functional local authority characterized by a hierarchical departmental structure where interdepartmental disputes

The case study represents a fictional authority. However, the author would like to thank Madeleine Knight and her colleagues in S.Tyneside Social Services Department for the invaluable advice and insights that they offered.

were common. Stourvale has a history of non-party rule and at present no political party has overall control. Its political make-up comprises Conservatives, Liberal Democrats and Independents; the Conservatives are in the majority but a number of committee chairs are held by the Liberal Democrats, including the Chair of Social Services.

Traditionally, the members have allowed the officers to be proactive in formulating policy, leaving the members to represent the interests of their particular wards. Members have long believed that their most important role is representing their constituents. Pressures on local government throughout the 1980s have forced the members to take a much more active interest in authority-wide issues and face up to the reality of reduced resources and the contract culture.

It will not be easy for them to come to a common view in determining the role of the local authority in community care. Some members interpret the 'enabling authority' as one where all contracts are given out to the private sector. Other members wish the authority to be involved in provision, while several of the Independents have strong links with the voluntary sector. The private sector has won a number of contracts including cleaning and catering in residential homes and day-care centres.

At the same time other services, such as education, will have a claim on any new resources. Traditionally Social Services, Housing and Education have not worked in a co-operative fashion.

The authority is coming under closer public scrutiny with Citizens Charter marks. There is an election due in May for one-third of the seats. Local government reorganization is very much on politicians' minds.

The local authority is committed to the provision of high-quality social services. The authority's mission statement recognizes that:

- services provided or purchased must respond to the assessed needs of the individuals who use them;
- such services need to be of the highest quality;
- services should be easily accessible to all irrespective of age, disability, race, religion or gender;
- services should be monitored to ensure quality and appropriateness.

The Social Services Department is increasingly a purchaser rather than a provider of services. In the past the Social Services Department has been a traditional bureaucratic local authority department characterized by empire building and interdepartmental rivalries. It has little experience of getting 'close to the customer', of contracting out services, or of management development. Market philosophy has not had an impact upon the department.

The senior management team responsible for drawing up the community care proposals has thus to ensure that it has in place the appropriate organizational structures, processes and personnel as well as the appropriate mechanisms for collaboration, consultation and co-ordination with other stakeholders. Traditionally, managers tend to have professional qualifications such as the Certificate of Qualification in Social Work (CQSW) rather than Master of Business Administration (MBA). Front-line managers are rarely consulted about changes and feel that their views are often ignored.

Stourvale Social Services Department has a budget of £30 million which is approximately 15 per cent of Stourvale's total budget. Of that £30 million approximately £15 million is used for other Social Service Department activities, particularly those concerned with the care of children. The current budget of Stourvale, 1994–5, for spending on community care, is therefore £15 million. Appendix 7.2, Tables 7.1–7.5 show how the money is spent.

The Council is reluctant to impose a high council tax but will consider charging for the services it provides.

Stourvale Social Services Department is divided into three districts:

1 *Western District* Geographically the largest, but with the smallest population. It is predominantly rural and includes a coastal region. It is popular with the elderly and is considered a retirement area. Transport facilities are poor and there is only one day centre for the elderly.
2 *Central District* This district has a higher population and is considered a desirable place to live. It is mostly suburban with good facilities and it is inhabited mainly by young families.
3 *Eastern District* The smallest in size but the most densely populated in three large towns. The towns are a mixture of Victorian terraced housing, with certain areas run down, modern flats for the single employed and council estates. The population is a mixture of age groups and ethnic minority groups. There is a substantial elderly Asian population who traditionally have not used social services facilities.

Appendix 7.3 provides background information on Stourvale's demographic features.

Relations with stakeholders

The relations between the Social Services Department and other organizations and agencies in the area has been mixed.

1 With the *voluntary sector*, relations have been distant. Some money is
   given to voluntary groups, particularly those who organize Meals-on-
   Wheels. The local authority has never monitored this expenditure.

   Locally, the voluntary sector has been concerned with advocacy and
   has been dominated by members of the middle class. It has traditionally
   provided transport, luncheon clubs, sitting services and help in day
   centres. There has been a lack of organization and no one body to
   represent the interests of the voluntary sector as a whole. Because of
   this lack of organization the voluntary sector has had little access to the
   decision-making forums of the statutory agencies other than support
   from individual members of the Council. Traditionally, the voluntary
   sector's strengths are seen as altruism, the absence of professional values, the absence of overt political viewpoints, accessibility to citizens,
   informality and cheapness. There is little information available of the
   contractual specifications that the local authority might adopt in terms
   of quality, evaluation or different types of contract. It is likely that
   different stakeholders will have different definitions of quality.

   A group has now been formed to bring together voluntary groups
   in the area and this group believes that the community care proposals
   give the voluntary sector an opportunity to be more proactive, to widen
   the scope of its activities and to achieve a higher profile in the local
   community. In addition local branches of national organizations such
   as MIND and MENCAP are looking to make more of an impact at
   local level.

2 With the *private sector* the local authority has not had good relations in
   this field. One large company provides a majority of the residential care
   for the elderly and is considered to provide a reasonable service. However, in the past three to four years a large number of small independent residential homes have sprung up and some provide a questionable
   service. The local authority has failed to keep up with this growth and
   many of these small operators have not been inspected or monitored.

   Private sector involvement in the provision of local authority services
   in Stourvale has been fairly limited. However, one large company primarily involved in residential care for the elderly has a large share of
   the market. This company is dubious about the profitability of other
   areas of community care and it envisages barriers to entry. Similarly,
   other private sector organizations are unlikely, without inducements,
   to bid for contracts for other than residential care for the elderly. One
   other company is, however, looking to form strategic alliances to enter

other markets. This company has already won contracts from the local authority to provide cleaning and catering services in local authority residential homes and day centres.

There are likely to be opportunities for private sector organizations to exploit. It is anticipated that growth areas will be day-care provision and respite care. Changes in legislation means that even in residential care the business will not be as profitable in the future. In the past social security payments, which were more generous than local authority rates, made residential homes a profitable business. Under the new arrangements the local authority purchases the service from the providers.

The nature of future arrangements with the local authority are unclear and there is little available information on contractual specifications in terms of quality, unit size, evaluation and the different forms of contract. In addition different definitions of quality are likely to exist.

3   With the *local health authority* relations have been distant. In theory, joint funding is available but neither Stourvale nor the health authority have had much interest in developing joint initiatives.

In 1991 the Government introduced a programme of reform within the National Health Service and NHS trusts were created along with GP fundholders. The purchaser–provider split was introduced and GP fundholders can purchase services from several providers including NHS trusts. In Stourvale there are four GP fundholders serving 30 per cent of the population. There is one trust – Stourvale Health Care Trust set up in 1993. In Stourvale the District Health Authorities and the Family Health Service Authorities have established the Stourvale Health Commission which acts as the purchaser of community-based health care. It can purchase services from neighbouring areas. The Health Commission has a budget of £1 million for the purchase of care in the community. At present there are no plans to increase this figure.

Traditionally, the medical profession is extremely powerful and is committed to high-profile medical care. Most resources go into acute care with community care a real Cinderella service.

There has been little commitment to management training and most clinicians are sceptical of management skills. Because of resource constraints one hospital is due to close with long-stay patients having to move to residential or nursing homes in the community.

4. Traditionally *users and carers* have had little impact on the services that have been delivered to them. This group of people have traditionally little power and no access to decision-making processes. They have

little confidence in their ability to get their views known and have been ignored by the statutory agencies. Their knowledge of what is available is usually limited.

A group of families has got together to try and influence the decision-making process but has little experience of advocacy or of articulating its views. Informal carers traditionally are isolated, need respite on a regular basis and are usually women. There is an absence of help outside normal office hours. The group is concerned that resources will be allocated according to what the Social Services Department thinks it has available rather than on the basis of need. It also wants consultation and not merely information.

5. The *Housing Department* has to prepare its strategy for 1994/5 and thereafter. It is required to show specifically how the demand for housing from people with special needs will be met. The Standard Spending Assessment for 1994–5 is down 3.5 per cent over 1993/4. Capital grants are at a post-war low in real terms. The Housing Management Function must be exposed to competitive tender by October 1997.

Right-to-buy has been popular and almost 35 per cent of the stock has been sold. Houses with gardens have been the most popular with buyers. All sheltered accommodation has been handed over to a local housing association. There is no foreseeable prospect of all single parent families currently on the waiting list being housed in the next ten years. Election manifestos of all parties contain pledges to remedy this. The local branch of Shelter is campaigning on this issue.

Homelessness has been increasing. The department has a policy of not using bed and breakfast accommodation except as a last resort. This puts considerable pressure on such temporary accommodation as is available, e.g. voids, and the situation could get worse. New building starts are the lowest since 1963. Several staff are members of the Institute of Housing. The Director is a member of the Chief Officers Management Team.

Morale within the department is fragile, especially in the 'front-line' services. Citizens Charter targets are not being met fully.

All the bodies involved in community care planning are committed to joint working and planning. A Joint Consultative Committee formed from members of the local authority and the Health Commission meet regularly. Consideration is being given to set up joint planning teams to look after specific client groups. There are obstacles, however, arising from historical and traditional differences in training and approach.

One of the tasks of the Joint Consultative Committee was to seek to improve the information to users and carers. The committee has published 15 leaflets in five different languages indicating what services are available.

Further information is also available through GPs surgeries and through the Health Care Trust. The Social Services Department is seeking other ways to make sure that people are better informed about community care.

Implementing Community Care

Implementing community care requires managers to develop new skills: managing contracts, assessing need, working with other agencies, handling budgets and so on.

I believe a good manager is a good manager, whatever discipline they come from. But there is an important element in managing social services that involves caring, and I would always want to see that mixture is there. I would prefer to have a social work practitioner, and provide the financial tools to play the part. (Local Authority deputy director)

An enabling role to my mind requires in some ways a higher degree of management skill than a providing role because it calls for a real concentration on the precise content of contracts or arrangements with third parties. It requires clarification of the outputs expected from the contract in the sense of clarity as to the quality to be achieved, standards to be attained, as well as the financial aspects. It calls for real management understanding as to how to devolve responsibility effectively and to set local budgets. It calls for advocacy in the broadest sense of community needs through the planning process and more narrowly of individual needs in the assessment process. (Sir Roy Griffiths)

Stourvale is now implementing its community care strategy and after a difficult first year appears to be coping as well as could be expected given its problems in producing its strategy.

The views of different stakeholders are reproduced below.

Politicians

We were far too slow in preparing for community care. We assumed that the Conservatives would lose the 1992 election and that a Labour government would rethink the whole idea. Our politicians are also interested in the nuts-and-bolts and not in the airy-fairy of trying to formulate a strategy.

It is yet another attempt to reduce the power of local authorities. How can you have market principles determining care. The market might be OK for street cleaning or leisure but surely not for caring for the needy?

Unfortunately there is an increasing concentration of people who are dependent upon state and council benefits and services, especially the very elderly who require intensive care and support.

Money is always tight but I believe that if we introduced a system of charging for, say, use of day centres, or do more in the way of means testing then the problem of lack of resources will lessen.

Citizens charters and patient charters raise expectations about the services but, as usual, central government does not give us the money to deliver high quality services.

Senior Manager

I don't think money is the problem. In fact the government has just announced an extra £20 million. The problem we have is that we can't spend all our allocation. We now have to spend 85 per cent in the Independent Sector and quite frankly the supply is just not there.

To be honest it is the information systems, or lack of them, that causes the problems. The financial systems that we had in place were antiquated and nothing was ever costed properly. More importantly though we had no idea of what was being provided and by whom. We have had to get information from the health authorities, voluntary sector and private sector as well as individual users and carers. To co-ordinate all this has proven a nightmare. It is also difficult getting the right information to the right level.

Social Services Director

Quite frankly we were not ready for community care. Nevertheless we have made great strides in the past year. The problem is we are still practising crisis management. It only takes one Ben Silcock and the publicity is unremitting. Whoever said that managing public services is all about managing in a goldfish bowl was absolutely right.

The government can speak the language of quality, developing a market for community care, the enabling authority, etc. but it is fairly meaningless when it comes to implementing changes. What we need is time and resources. Time to train people, to understand the legislation, to change the whole culture of this organization. As usual government with its eyes on the next election wants everything to happen overnight.

Social Services Contracts Manager

Its been a nightmare – half my staff have not received any training. The guidelines were quickly drawn up and we are all terrified of conflicts of interest and stepping over the boundaries of probity. Some of our colleagues in the health service see nothing wrong with accepting gifts from providers – they have been doing it for years with the drug companies. For us accusations of corruption have to be taken seriously.

Care Manager 1

I am between a rock and a hard place. On the one hand I am trying to put together a menu of care but I don't have any authority over budgets or contracts. If I want to purchase a particular care package I have to refer upwards to the contracts manager. Its very frustrating.

Care Manager 2

I have social work qualifications and I did not come into this job to act as a resource rationer. There is no way that we have a needs-led service. As usual it depends upon the resources available.

Care Manager 3

Its all very well for the Department and the local health authority to preach about the virtues of joint planning but when it comes to the crunch its the GPs who I have to deal with and they have the money and the power.

Area Team Leader 1

I am spending more and more time running a budget than managing the job. As it is my team is struggling to keep up with the case load. Devolving budgets is all very well but we don't have the time or the expertise to do financial assessments and work out the individual user needs. I am lucky in having a dedicated team – we get by on good will.

Area Team Leader 2

I quite like having control over my own budget. It allows me to make decisions and gives me some flexibility. There is a perception that social workers can't and shouldn't control budgets and I suppose that my management diploma has taught me not to be afraid of figures.

Area Team Leader 3

My team might just be able to keep on top of assessments. But there is a real problem of monitoring the quality of provision and I don't know what the solution is. We just don't have the time to assess the quality of every residential or day centre place and there are no national guidelines to help us. How do you define quality of life?

Mentally ill patient

When the hospital closed down what was I supposed to do? Sleep on the streets? OK the hostel is a pig-sty, the owner is a crook and there is over-crowding. But Social Services can't get its act together: it takes too long to do the assessment, it's too bureaucratic and there ain't enough accommo-dation anyway.

Local authority training manager

We try and bring together managers from different backgrounds with dif-ferent expertise in, for example, physical disability or people with learning difficulties. For example we ran a two-day course on assessment and care planning for a mix of field social workers, hospital social workers, occupa-tional therapists and home care organizer.

Local authority training manager 2

Its all very well working up these elaborate plans and strategies: they require a fundamental change in the culture of the organization. You need training and development to achieve this. Yet training is always the first budget to be hit.

Carer 1

It's impossible to work out who is responsible for what. It seems to me that the only difference between a health care bath and a social care bath is that you put Dettol in one and bubble bath in the other. Trying to get informa-tion on what is available and from whom is very difficult.

Carer 2

Its so confusing. There have been so many changes its impossible to keep up. All you hear is 'we are a purchaser not a provider' and 'we are not contracted to do this'. In the old days you knew who was providing help and you built up a relationship of trust with them.

Carer 3

Despite the rhetoric of putting our needs and those in our care first, I found some of the staff still patronizing – its the 'we know best' attitude and they make assumptions without really listening.

Carer 4

We have a reputation for looking after our own. The family is very important to us. But we can't always cope. The younger ones no longer are prepared to look after their grandparents or even parents like we did before. OK so the information is printed in Urdu but they do not really understand the needs of our community. I do know that the post of Ethnic Rights Officer has been vacant for some time.

Health Authority Manager

On the whole we now have good relations with our counterparts in social services. Yet they are still too bureaucratic: we are keen to increase the throughput and improve our efficiency. Quite frankly social services just takes too long in assessment and beds are being blocked. Not only that but the committee cycle in local government does not lend itself to quick decision making.

District nurse

We are getting there. At first I used to resent all the bureaucracy, like filling in forms for someone to get a disabled car drivers badge. But I recognize that home care staff are just as anxious that the patient or the client is at the centre of what we do and it doesn't matter who delivers the service. I am working closer with the social workers and on the ground we get things done. The problem is higher up where there is a lot of political in-fighting between the GPs and the hospitals, between senior managers in the local authority and the Health Commission.

Housing managers (local authority)

Nobody ever really thought about our contribution to community care. We have been marginalized. Social Services don't appear to be aware of our problems. We can't build new houses, we are under pressure from CCT and yet they want us to spend our budget on aids, adaptations, home support and so on without ever thinking to consult with us.

Voluntary sector volunteer

I started volunteer work because I wanted to make a contribution to the community around me. I know it sounds do-gooding but I wanted to help people. Now we are run like a business – its all about value-for-money, fulfilling contracts, controlling budgets. Some of my colleagues welcome this. They think that it gives us greater status and we are no longer totally reliant on grants. But we still need donations, and 'give us a fiver: a director of finance and a personnel director to support' does not have quite the same ring to it.

User 1

I think that community care is a great idea. For the first time, I feel that Social Services are beginning to take me seriously. In the past the attitude has been 'aren't these people lucky to receive our services'!.

User 2

Its not much to ask for – somebody to collect my pension and do the cleaning and ironing. All I want is a guaranteed service, having a choice of who does it is irrelevant to me.

User 3

I get sick of the 'office hours' mentality'. I want a service that is convenient for me, not for the local authority. They don't really understand what it is like to be disabled.

Private Sector 1

Its all very well pushing for spot contracts. I agree that this is the most flexible for the user. But what guarantees do we have? For small operators it creates uncertainty. We would much rather have block contracts where places are bought in advance. It gives us some stability and helps us in our planning and secures our immediate future while we come to terms with this new climate.

Private Sector 2

Our residential care business is doing well; local authorities no longer resent us and where we have poor relations it is often because some politicians are reluctant to give up the provider role and they mistrust our profit motive. On the other hand, domiciliary care is, quite frankly, not worth our while even though local authorities are keen to develop this aspect of community care. Different authorities use different accounting procedures; and there are too many restrictions on our staffing policy imposed by local authority contracts.

Private Sector 3

Quite frankly I think that there is over-provision in residential care. With stricter monitoring of homes and with the reduction in income following on from the money being switched from Social Security to the local authority, there will be a shakeout and some homes will go under.

Discussion Questions

1 What appear to be the major problems in implementing community care?

2 How can Stourvale ensure that its implementation strategy is consistent with its vision for community care?

3 How can the demands of different stakeholders be reconciled?

Background Note

The concept of Care in the Community has been with us for some time. For the past three decades politicians, academics and practitioners have felt that certain types of care are best carried out in the community rather than in institutions. Thus, care of the elderly, mentally ill, mentally handicapped and the physically disabled have all been subject to scrutiny for Care in the Community. A good example of this approach has been the All Wales Strategy, initiated in 1983, which was committed to giving people with mental handicaps a normal pattern of life within the community.

The most recent expression of Care in the Community is the National Health Service and Community Care Act 1990 which gives legislative effect to the proposals first put forward in Sir Roy Griffiths, *Community Care: Agenda for Action*, following on from an Audit Commission report of *Making a Reality of Community Care*. The main recommendations of the Griffiths report included:

• primary responsibility for community care should lie with local authorities;
• collaboration between local authorities and the health service should precede the presentation of plans to the Minister for Community Care;
• local authority social service departments should be re-oriented towards the design and co-ordination of packages of care largely provided by others.

The report suggested that a mixed bag of provision should be encouraged where agencies from the private and voluntary sectors actually provided the service. Thus the concept of welfare pluralism was used to indicate how different bodies should be involved in the provision of community care. The responsibility of the local authority was to set local priorities, design individual packages of care, arrange delivery and make maximum use of the private and voluntary sectors. The local authority was to act as an enabling authority. The principles of the Griffiths Report were endorsed by the Government insofar as it believed that such an approach would encourage consumer choice and flexibility, stimulate competition and improve efficiency and effectiveness in service delivery. The Government's views on community care were, then, no different to its views on the rest of local authority activities.

The Act itself recommended:

1 that local authorities be given major responsibility for providing and/ or organizing social care for the elderly, for the mentally ill and for those who have physical or learning disabilities;
2 that responsibility for the funding of residential care for elderly people and others be transferred to local government from the Department of Social Security;
3 that a case management and assessment system be introduced to which all of those likely to need community care will be entitled and through which they must pass to be eligible for certain publicly funded services;

4   that a comprehensive planning system for community care be developed in consultation with other authorities such as health, housing and voluntary organizations;
5   that an arms-length inspectorate be introduced to monitor standards in local authority residential care as well as the independent residential sector;
6   that a statutory complaints procedure be instituted;
7   that a specific grant to accelerate development of the mental illness services be introduced;
8   that the emphasis for local authorities be on purchasing rather than directly providing services.

The Act did not endorse the view put forward in the Griffiths Report that monies for community care should be ring-fenced. However, this has since changed.

The Government proposed that money would be transferred from the social security budget to local authorities. Previously Social Security paid for residential care for those in private sector residential homes. Local authorities resented this as social security payment was invariably higher than local authority payment and many felt that the private sector made a 'killing'.

Originally, £539 million, all ring-fenced, was to be provided for community care of which £399 million would be transferred from Social Security and £140 million will be new money for one year only. Local authorities argued that this was insufficient and would lead to a shortfall of some £200 million and that 12,000 elderly and disabled people would be at risk of not getting the care services they require. This funding has since been increased.

The Government also announced that 75 per cent of this money would have to be spent on care in the independent sector.

The original proposals were to be introduced in April 1991. However, the Government later decided on a phased implementation in three stages over two years:

1   By April 1991:

    •   the establishment of inspection units for residential care homes which is independent of day-to-day management;
    •   the introduction of specific grants for people with mental health problems and for people who have drug or alcohol abuse problems;
    •   the introduction of comprehensive complaints procedures.

2 By April 1992:

   • the publication of community care plans which take the form
     of joint planning agreements with other organizations including
     health authorities, service users and carers, the voluntary and private
     sectors;
   • preparatory work to introduce a unified assessment procedure for
     people in need of community care support;
   • preparatory work to introduce a case management scheme for peo-
     ple whose service needs are complex.

3 By April 1993:

   • a unified assessment procedure in place;
   • a care management scheme fully introduced which includes care
     planning and the regular review of people's needs.

At the heart of the proposals is a move away from a service-centred to a
needs-led approach to community care. Historically, the service provided
has depended on the funds available, determined partly by political choice,
and by the *perceived* needs of the population. The Audit Commission Bulletin
'Taking Stock: Progress with Community Care', argues that a needs-led
approach requires authorities to be more 'sensitive, flexible and responsive'.
Being more sensitive requires a clearer understanding of the numbers requiring help and the type of help they require. Greater flexibility requires
operational arrangements that allow local managers to respond to individual
needs quickly. Being more responsive recognizes the diversity of need and
that new patterns of care may be appropriate.
   The achievement of a more sensitive, flexible and responsive approach
will partly depend on funding arrangements, and Appendix 7.1 provides
information on these.
   Commentators on the changes to the provision of community care raise
a number of issues.

The issues

What is community care?   What do we mean by community care and is
there general agreement on what it should encompass? Different groups
may have different perceptions so that we might find a definition of health
care in competition with social care. Where are the boundaries between

them? A further definitional problem is that the concept of community care assumes that there is something called 'the community' out there. It may well be that some areas/neighbourhoods are more sympathetic to the disabled than others. This is an important consideration if the aim of community care is to integrate individuals back into a community.

Who is to provide it? Not all local authorities go along with the concept of the enabling authority that is in use, i.e. acting as a purchaser rather than a provider. For political/ideological reasons some authorities do not see their roles in the same way. Similarly, what happens if there does not exist the private sector or voluntary sector to undertake the work? The assumption is that there are a host of other agencies that are able and willing to provide the service. The voluntary sector may have a tradition of advocacy and may be unwilling to get involved in large-scale direct provision. Similarly, the private sector might find providing residential care for the elderly to be attractive but may be less interested in providing services for highly dependent people.

What will be its impact on existing provision? The proposals also require a profound shift from a services-led delivery to a needs-led delivery, needs which are notoriously difficult to define. In the All Wales Strategy for the Mentally Handicapped mentioned earlier it was often the case that rather than individual care packages being drawn up, the individual received what was available.

It will require a change in the role of local authorities which now have to:

• stimulate a mixed delivery;
• introduce competitive tendering and contracting out;
• introduce cost-centre management and devolved budgeting;
• introduce resource management systems;
• separate out the purchase and supply of services;
• establish key indicators and performance measurement.

It will also have an impact on the roles of professionals insofar as new skills of management will need to be developed by the medical profession, new skills of contract management by local authority officers and new skills of collaboration by all concerned. At the same time service users and informal carers will need to be articulate in their demands to ensure full use is made of consultation.

How will it be done? Joint planning and action is crucial. Does it exist already, is there a tradition of working together? At what stage should the voluntary sector be involved? The All Wales Strategy found problems here with the voluntary sector resenting their treatment as inferior partners by the statutory agencies involved.

At the very least we would expect there to be agreement on common goals, on defining needs, on priorities and on the implementation of a common strategy. The success depends on the interorganizational production of community care plans and the inter-professional production of individual care packages. We can legitimately ask: how do local authorities and health authorities collect, share and agree on basic information such as demography, dependency characteristics and the scale and scope of needs within geographical areas, particularly if there is no tradition of inter-agency collaboration?

The vehicle that drives the partnership approach must include trust, commitment and common goals.

Possible problems

1   What happens with market failure? Is the local authority in a position to provide the services itself?
2   In the event of the local authority giving up any commitment to service provision how does it deal with monopoly provision?
3   The private sector may be interested in providing a standard service for a mass market rather than individual care.
4   We must also consider the problems of yet more changes for the NHS to deal with. How much time and effort can the NHS devote to community care given all the other recent changes of internal markets, trust status etc.?
5   Will there be a tendency to discharge people early into the community to free beds or meet targets based on throughputs. This will place an increasing stress on community care.
6   How compatible are the organizational structures of the NHS and the local authority? Are they based on area, function or client group?
7   Will the voluntary sector be prepared to enter into contract agreements?

Despite the fact that community care has been in operation for two years many of the above issues and problems remain unresolved. Indeed new problems have arisen.

Appendix 7.1: Special Transitional Grant

Flexibility requires the ability of care managers to purchase services when and where necessary so it is important that money is available to 'spot' purchase. 1993–4 saw the introduction of the Special Transitional Grant (STG) which provided funds not assigned for specific services but available for flexible purchasing. The main purpose of the grant was to transfer responsibility for the funding of care from the social security system to local authority services. The Audit Commission (1994) has calculated that the STG now forms 21 per cent of the total social services budget; in 1993–4 that figure was 14 per cent.

The STG in brief:

1 STG in 1993–4 = £565 million; 1994–5 = £736 million.
2 Funds transferred from Social Security make up the largest element: 1993–4 = £339 million; 1994–5 = £652 million. Of this 85 per cent has to be spent on non-local authority services.
3 The allocation of STG to individual local authorities depends on the formula for distributing the overall block grant from central government and the number of people who were already being supported by social security benefits in independent homes.
4 This formula was changed in 1994–5 and is now wholly allocated according to the overall block grant. Some authorities gained and some lost.

Appendix 7.2: Stourvale Social Services Department

Table 7.1   Expenditure by client group 1994–1995

	£ million
Elderly	8
Mental health	0.7
Physical disability	2.5
Learning disability	3.8
	15

Table 7.2 Expenditure on elderly 1994–1995

	£ thousands
Residential care	3,500
Domiciliary care	2,000
Day centres	500
Day centres (voluntary sector)	500
Meals-on-wheels (private and voluntary)	500
Grants to voluntary sector	200
Management and support services	800
	8,000

Table 7.3 Expenditure on people with physical disabilities 1994–1995

	£ thousands
Residential care	450
Domiciliary care	500
Day centres	500
Occupational therapy	500
Grants to voluntary sector	300
Management and support services	250
	2,500

Table 7.4 Expenditure on mental health and illness 1994–1995

	£ thousands
Residential care	100
Domiciliary care	200
Specific grant for mental illness	250
Grants to voluntary sector	50
Management and support services	100
	700

Table 7.5   Expenditure on people with learning disabilities 1994–1995

	£ thousands
Residential care	1,000
Day centres	1,700
Domiciliary care	500
Grants to voluntary sector	250
Management and support services	350
	3,800

Table 7.6   Stourvale social services departments

Type of establishment	Number of establishments	Number of places
Homes for the elderly	10	420
Day centres for the elderly	5	200
Homes for adults with a learning disability	10	250
Day centres for adults with a learning disability	10	200
Homes for adults with a physical disability	2	70
Day centres for adults with a physical disability	5	160
Homes for people with a mental illness	1	20

Table 7.7   Private sector and voluntary establishments

Type of establishment	Number of establishments	Number of places
Homes for the elderly	22	540

Table 7.8   Location of social services departments' establishments

District	Type of establishment	Number of establishments	Number of places
Western	Homes for elderly	5	250
	Day centres for elderly	1	30
	Homes for adults with a learning disability	5	150
	Day centres for adults with a learning disability	3	70
	Home for adults with a physical disability	0	
	Day centres for adults with a physical disability	1	
	Homes for people with a mental illness	0	
Central	Homes for elderly	2	70
	Day centres for elderly	1	45
	Homes for adults with a learning disability	2	40
	Day centres for adults with a learning disability	3	55
	Home for adults with a physical disability	0	
	Day centres for adults with a physical disability	1	
	Homes for people with a mental illness	0	
Eastern	Homes for elderly	3	100
	Day centres for elderly	3	125
	Homes for adults with a learning disability	3	60
	Day centres for adults with a learning disability	4	
	Home for adults with a physical disability	2	
	Day centres for adults with a physical disability	3	
	Homes for people with a mental illness	1	

Appendix 7.3 Demographic Features of Stourvale

Stourvale consists of three distinct areas, comprising a rural, coastal region Western District; a suburban Central District; and an inner-city Eastern District. It has a population of 4,000,000.

There are several distinct population trends:

*   a reduction in the number of children and adults of working age;
*   an increase in the number of elderly people as a proportion of the overall population;
*   an increase in unemployment in Eastern District.

Table 7.9   People aged 65 years and above by district

District	% of people aged 65 and over
Western	25
Central	12
Eastern	20

Currently:

*   35 per cent of the population of Stourvale is wholly or mainly dependent on welfare benefits;
*   18 per cent of all households are dependent on income support;
*   35 per cent of all households contain at least one pensioner;
*   20 per cent of all households contain one or more persons with a long-term illness;
*   7 per cent of the population are registered with the Social Services Department as disabled;
*   non-whites account for 7 per cent of the population in the Eastern District.

Appendix 7.4 Glossary

Assessment   The process of defining need and determining eligibility for assistance against stated policy criteria. There are different levels of assessment depending on the complexity of need. It is a participative process involving the applicant, their carers and other relevant agencies.

Contracts   Agreements purchasing a range of services and facilities from a provider which are enforceable in law.

Care manager   Any practitioner who undertakes all, or most, of the core tasks of co-ordinating the assessment of a person's needs, who may carry budgetary responsibility but is not involved in any direct service provision.

Care package   A combination of service designed to meet the assessed needs of a person requiring care in the community.

Carers   Relatives and friends who provide support.

Day care   Communal care normally provided in a setting away from the user's place of residence, with paid or voluntary carers present. Day care can cover a wide range of services.

Discharge plan   Plans drawn up before a patient's discharge from hospital making appropriate arrangements for any necessary continuing care or treatment. The plans should include a checklist of action to be taken by all those concerned with the patient.

Enabling authority   An authority whose main function is to secure and fund services to reflect the assessed needs of its local population; selecting the most cost effective from among its own provision and that of other agencies.

Independent   Individuals, bodies or organizations not wholly con-
sector   trolled or maintained by a government department or any other authority or body instituted by Special Act of Parliament or incorporated by Royal Charter. The term may be taken to refer to the voluntary sector and the private sector.

| Purchaser/ provider split | Local authorities, for example, are encouraged not to directly provide services but to purchase services from a wider choice of providers including the voluntary sector and private sector. It is believed that this makes for greater choice and competition than if the local authority itself provided the services. |

References

Audit Commission, *Making a Reality of Community Care*, London: HMSO, 1988.
Audit Commission, 'Taking Stock: Progress with Community Care', London: HMSO, 1994.
Griffiths, R., Community Care: Agenda for Action, London: HMSO, 1988.

8

Wellcare Hospital Trust

ALAN LAWTON AND DAVID MCKEVITT

John Prideauz looked out of his office window to the beautifully manicured lawns below and to the executive car park beyond. He saw his own company Saab gleaming in the sunlight. All appeared to be well with the world. And yet John was a worried man. He had been in post as chief executive of the hospital for only a few months and the job was very different from what he had expected. He had been recruited from the private sector after a successful career in manufacturing. He had qualified as an engineer and later gained his MBA through part-time study. John formerly believed that running a hospital could not be that different from running a ball-bearing factory and had relished the challenge of improving the hospital's productivity, reducing its costs and making it more efficient. John had taken the job with firm views on how he could turn the organization around. After all, he had done it successfully on two occasions in the private sector. However, the financial figures for the previous six months made depressing reading and the lead story in his daily newspaper was about how many Trust hospitals had got into financial difficulties. Perhaps he had been over-confident, perhaps he had not realized the complexities of managing in the public sector. After idly wasting the first half-hour of his day with these thoughts he realized that he had better start being more constructive. He decided to review the progress he had made in the past few months and decide on his strategy for the future. Immediately, he realized that much of this time had been spent with day-to-day crises and with trying to defuse long-standing tensions between the different groups that made up the hospital's workforce. He decided to go back to basics and start from scratch. John pulled out the briefing papers he had been given prior to his appointment. They contained information about the hospital, and about the NHS (see Appendix 8.1). At the time it had seemed fairly straightforward but he realized that the complexities of organizational life in the NHS were far greater than he had imagined.

John thought that the key to improved performance lay in setting out clear targets and measuring their achievement. He decided to have a more thorough examination of the existing system for measuring performance and turned to a series of papers that had been produced by one of his middle managers. He recalled that the middle manager had carried out only the first part of an investigation into performance measurement. She had left the hospital shortly before John's arrival, under something of a cloud. Apparently she had kicked up a fuss about lack of co-operation and had committed the cardinal sin of criticizing the medical staff for not taking performance measurement seriously. She was seen as something of a trouble-maker but John did know that she was now working for another Trust hospital and was seen as a rising star. Appendix 8.2 contains a summary of her report on the performance measurement systems currently used by Wellcare Hospital. John did remember asking whether the investigation was continuing and was given an evasive reply by one of his senior managers.

John had always believed in MBWA (Management By Walking About) and felt that he needed to have a higher profile among all staff in the hospital. He realized that he still did not have a real feel for how the hospital worked and felt that informal chats with staff would give a sense of how people felt about the performance of the hospital. Reproduced below are some of the comments he received.

Perspectives on Performance Measurement

Consultants

All this paperwork erodes clinical time!

The current system needs to be bespoke rather than externally imposed.

We will need a strong executive lead on this.

There is pressure on managers to reduce costs without regard to effectiveness.

Performance measures are a paper exercise and just used to increase the political profile of the Trust: internally they are frequently used as a tool in the allocation of resources by powerful interests.

The only performance measurement that is worth anything is peer review. I don't want some jumped-up MBA telling me that my performance could be improved. Only my colleagues have the knowledge to comment on that.

Nurses

It is difficult measuring individual performance since it is so difficult working out who actually owns it. Patients well-being is dependent upon so many different people from the medical staff, to the porters, the ambulance crews or the social workers who look after them when they leave here.

There are league tables for hospital performance (waiting lists, times etc) but the system still isn't truly responsive to the patient's needs.

Attitudes must change, such that doctors do not see themselves as all-important and managers see that they have greater control. Many of the barriers to entry of the profession remain. Such change is definitely seen as unacceptable from the doctor's perspective.

Target setting is currently only for arrival contacts with patients or for waiting times at appointment.

Most staff are indifferent to the current performance measures. They bear little resemblance to the service delivered, they are time consuming and provide minimal feedback to the staff.

Whatever system we use it must reflect the care and attention that we give to individual patients. It must also reflect the complexity of individual patient needs.

Middle managers

Technical barriers can be overcome but the behavioural barriers are still present.

Most stakeholders view the Government, closely followed by consultants, as the most powerful and patients and their representatives as least powerful.

I want to know how well neighbouring OPDs perform in terms of overall budget, activity and quality because this will help me develop a marketing strategy to influence purchasers.

I want to influence directly those groups of patients most likely to seek a choice of hospital such as pregnant mothers or those seeking non-emergency treatment.

If quality is defined as the ability to satisfy need, it begs the question of whether this is felt (expressed) need or expertly defined (normative) need. Measures of expressed need can be tapped in a variety of ways – not simply the patients complaints and satisfaction surveys, but also user forums or panels lead by 'neutral' facilitators. The former methods are easily quantified, but can fail to tap much opinion that the patient may not express to staff in fear of adverse influence on their care and general loyalty to the NHS, or low expectations.

The acceptability of patient satisfaction feedback data collected by patients organizations is more threatening to hospital staff than in-house data collection, precisely because it can be less easily biased in favour of the hospital.

There is a weakness in the current arrangements in deciding *who* should be monitoring performance – the providers or the purchasers.

Networking, collaboration, co-operation and communication have to be improved among all stakeholders if performance assessment in the public domain is to be improved.

The current systems are the result of demands from central government departments or oganizational management needs. Even with the Patients Charter monitoring standards are selected centrally rather than based on users local interest.

The trust will need to provide a proven value for money, quality service that is responsive to the GPs needs. Failure to do so will inevitably lead to a loss of business. The role of PIs to prove effectiveness should not be underestimated in this process.

Greater emphasis must now be placed on making both financial and information systems more accurate because in future the commissioners will be basing contracts on such information and this will affect the ultimate *survival* of the Trust. Professionals must recognize this and managers must be flexible to allow more time to be spent on information collection. This could lead to a small increase in admin and clerical staff who are normally used to collate and record such information.

Accurate information is required by both sides: the purchaser needs a clear idea of what services it requires: the provider needs to know how much and when it is required to provide.

Performance indicators usually mean reducing costs at any price without any thought given to effectiveness.

Unlike in business, I do not know who my customers are. Is it those who use us, is it the medical staff, is it the community generally? It is not just the patient.

Stakeholders

John realized that the views expressed were fairly selective and represented only the internal stakeholders of the hospital. He quickly drew up a list of all the possible stakeholders and tried to think through what their interests might be:

Stakeholders	*Possible interests*
Nurses	Patient care, interesting job, career progression
Patients	Better health!
Doctors	Quality of care, career progression, research
GPs	Quality and cost of care
Managers	Costs, efficiency, patient satisfaction, level of competition, business growth
Government	Costs, avoid possible scandals, leagues tables of performance
Health authority	Costs, equitable treatment, league tables and comparisons, access
Local politicians	Avoid scandals, no hospital closures
Professional bodies	Quality of health; protection of members and maintenance of standards.
Trust board	Survival, achieve a surplus, levels of remuneration.

John recognized that not all of these interests could be reconciled and that performance measurement might mean different things to different people. He also recognized that the brief summary of the current system of performance indicators (Appendix 8.2) left much room for improvement. He dug out his notes from a conference he had recently attended on performance measurement in the public services (Appendix 8.3).

John was left reflecting that in the 'new' NHS, the internal market would judge performance. Hospitals which provided an effective and efficient service which gave the customer what he or she wanted would survive and prosper. Those that did not would go under. Whether or not this would be politically acceptable, John had his doubts but managers had to recognize that they were running a business. In this new world, the purchaser was of crucial importance as GPs, for example, sought to get the best value for money from the providers for their patients. Fundholders were key players in the market and they were becoming adept at exploiting their new strengths.

Managing in the NHS was all about being responsive to the customer and managers had to be flexible in response to consumer demands. However, John was beginning to appreciate that the manager's hands were often tied in crucial areas of performance. The power of the professional bodies had made it difficult to move to a more flexible pay system which allowed him to pay for good performance and to penalize poor performance. Certainly the Government was reluctant to be seen to be battering the nurses.

Discussion Questions

1 What would you recommend as a new performance measurement system for Wellcare?

2 How would you recommend that John Prideaux satisfy the needs of the different stakeholders?

3 How can quality of health service be defined?

Appendix 8.1: The Changing National Health Service

Wellcare Trust Hospital is an acute general hospital with 300 beds. It has 20,000 outpatients per year. It is structured into clinical directorates comprising obstetrics/gynaecology, general surgery, orthopaedics and trauma, paediatrics and general medicines.

The percentage spent on administrative costs is slightly higher than the national average. The physical quality of the buildings is poor and will need extensive refurbishment.

There is one other Trust hospital 20 miles away and four district general hospitals in the next district.

The Trust is run by a board of directors, the chairperson being appointed by the Government and with a number of local businessmen on the board. The board can run the Trust as an independent business and has the powers to determine staff levels and mix and can negotiate outputs with a variety of purchasers with whom it enters into contracts.

The Trust's Mission Statement is: 'To provide high quality healthcare across the full spectrum of general hospital services to its local population. That care must be patient-centred.'

The NHS has undergone profound changes in its structure, financing and operating environment in recent years. The major piece of legislation introducing these changes was the National Health Service and Community Care Act 1990. The Act was intended to bring about the introduction of market-like mechanisms into the NHS through the separation of the providers of health care from the purchasers. The relationship between the purchasers and providers was to be regulated through the use of contracts. The reform would, it was argued, allow purchasers to shop around to get the best deal from providers, increasing choice and ensuring that competition improved efficiency.

The purchasers of health care would be the District Health Authorities and General Practitioner (GP) fundholders. GP practices of a certain size were allowed to control their own budgets and purchase health care for their patients. Other possible purchasers include insurance companies and employers.

The providers of health care were classified as those hospitals directly managed by the health authority and a new breed of hospital Trusts. Trusts are independent self-managed units run by a board staffed by government appointees and representatives of the medical profession. A Trust can retain its financial surpluses and invest in the business. It has flexibility over levels of remuneration and the numbers and mix of staff.

Other providers may include ambulance or community services. Purchasers can buy health care from neighbouring districts if they so desire. Funding for purchasers is determined, partly, on a capitation basis depending on the number of patients on a GPs list or the size of the resident population.

The intention is to place patient interests above those of the providers and alongside the Patients Charter which defines the service that patients can expect to make a public service more responsive to the needs of its 'customers'.

Appendix 8.2: Wellcare's Performance Indicators

Performance indicators in the NHS were introduced in the 1980s and concentrated on activity levels. Performance indicators were concerned with increasing the number of, for example, open heart operations or hip replacement operations; other indicators measured cost per case treated, staffing levels related to patient numbers, waiting lists and so on. Early performance indicators were criticized for using already generated statistics and 'rebadging' them, for concentrating on throughput rather than outcome and for not measuring quality.

Critics have argued that performance indicators were issued as a control mechanism by central government to ensure the economic use of taxpayers' money.

Wellcare's current system of performance indicators focuses on:

- cost of staff;
- cancelled appointments;
- waiting times;
- attendances;
- non-attendances;
- number of clinics per 1,000 population;
- budget statements;
- complaints;
- workload.

A major problem that Wellcare faces is lack of information. We tend to 'rebadge' statistics collected for different purposes and call them performance indicators. Managers lack basic financial data to make decisions. If we are serious about pushing responsibility downwards then we have to allow managers the 'freedom to manage'. Part of this involves making financial decisions: they cannot do this if they do not have the basic information concerning the costs of operations, X-rays, equipment, etc.

Nurses are frustrated because they cannot get quick access to patients records. We installed the new computer system but did not spend enough time training nurses on how to use it.

Consultants resent what they see as yet another encroachment on their territory by managers who do not have medical expertise.

Increasingly the nature of our business will be governed by contracts with purchasers. We need to develop skills in contract management as performance targets will be an integral part of the 'contract culture'. At present most contracts are likely to be block contracts in which we receive an annual fee in return for a broad range of services and which are measured in terms of length of stay, waiting lists, and so on. Quality is not clearly specified. We can expect, however, pressure to move to cost-per-case contracts where quality and targets are much more clearly specified and costed.

Appendix 8.3: Performance Indicators in the Public Sector

Can be used to:

1   clarify objectives;
2   evaluate outcomes;
3   input into incentive schemes and staff appraisal;
4   enable consumers to make informed choices;
5   indicate standards and allow monitoring;
6   calculate the contribution of different activities to overall performance;
7   spotlight problem areas;
8   help in cost-benefit analysis;
9   indicate potential areas of cost reduction.

Six Dimensions of Quality in Health Care

1   Access to services
2   Relevance to need
3   Effectiveness
4   Equity
5   Social acceptability
6   Efficiency and economy

Criteria for Performance Indicators

1   Timeliness
2   Accuracy

3   Acceptability
4   Suitability
5   Feasibility
6   Usefulness
7   Consistency
8   Comparability
9   Clarity
10 Controllability
11 Availability

Dimensions of Performance Measurement

Structure	Process	Outcome
Inputs	Activity	Outputs
Economy	Efficiency	Effectiveness

QUALITY

9

Networking in Wales: European Regional Development Fund and Welsh Office– Local Authority Relations*

RUSSELL DEACON AND ALAN LAWTON

This case examines the process through which the European Regional Development Fund (ERDF) was administered within Wales prior to local government reorganization. In particular, the relationships between the stakeholders, the European Commission, the Welsh Office and local authorities within Wales are investigated. The case considers these relationships from the perspective of a network analysis and discusses the extent to which the traditional relationship between central and local government in the UK has been supplanted by the tripartite relationship involving the European Commission. The case focuses on the allocation of the ERDF and the Background Note (pp. 164–7) provides the detail of the mechanics of the fund and describes some of the intentions behind the Commission's regional policy. The case illustrates the characteristics of networks that managers need to be aware of if the implementation of policies that cut across organizational boundaries is to be successful.

Centre–Local Relations in Wales

Traditionally relations between central government and local government in the UK have been described in terms of central government being the

* This case draws upon interviews with Welsh Office officials and local government officers in Wales.

senior partner, or of local government as an agent of central government and dependent on it. The relationship has been seen in hierarchical terms. More recently, the concept of a network has been used to describe relations between different parts of government since a network of relationships, both personal and organizational, is said to be dynamic and illustrates inter-dependencies and the complexity of such interdependencies. A network can be described as a set of relationships that exists within and across organizations involving both formal and informal channels and existing at different levels within and across organizations. Such relationships may be between individuals or groups and will exist over time. Participants in such networks will expect to gain some advantages from belonging to the network. Thus, in the context of central – local relationships, central government may wish to enhance political and economic stability and system maintenance by interacting with local government. At the same time local authorities will anticipate having their interests taken into consideration when policy is being formulated or resources are being allocated. Networks are said to capture the 'multiple, complex, dynamic and continous' character of centre–local relations. Each participant will have its own autonomy determined by different resources, and bargaining and compromise will feature strongly.

There are a number of features that characterize networks.

Context

In recent years the Welsh Office has been at the heart of governance within Wales. It is typically described as looking to represent the interests of Wales in Westminster and the interests of Westminster in Wales. As a territorial department it acts as a one-stop shop so that it performs functions that in England would fall under functional departments. As far as local government is concerned the Welsh Office will deal with different parts of local government depending on the issue. It is likely to have extensive links with local authorities spread across a number of policy areas. It is likely that the general relationship between local authorities and the Welsh Office will also obtain in the case of ERDF. Implementation of ERDF will take place within a general context of central–local government relations. The strength and form of these relationships has developed over time and expectations as to future relationships will follow on from previous relationships. In Wales it is argued that a closeness has developed not just because of its functions but also because of the relatively small number of local authorities in Wales, i.e. prior to reorganization, eight counties and 37 districts. This means that informal personal links have developed. There is a perception, particularly held by the Welsh Office, that Wales operates a system of 'good government' in the sense that strong relationships exist between local authorities and the Welsh Office which facilitate decision making.

Centrality

Network analysts consider that the more central the position in the network the more important the member. The position of centrality may be taken by the strategy maker. A defining feature will be control over resources. Another feature may be autonomy so that the relationship between members of a network may be influenced by how much they depend on each other. The reformed ERDF gave central government in member states a central role so that the process is heavily influenced by the centre, in this case the Welsh Office. The Welsh Office is responsible for advising local authorities on the eligibility of their submissions and for assessing these submissions. In acting as a sieve the Welsh Office may save local authorities unnecessary time and expenditure in submitting ineligible projects. However, the local authority is unable to appeal against any rejections. If local authorities are dissatisfied with the Welsh Office's view on a particular project, they are able to raise their objections to rulings on eligibility with the programme monitoring committee. Critics argue that the Welsh Office can constitute the biggest hurdle that local authorities have to climb in applying for regional aid.

Expertise and information

Is it possible for one group to dominate a network because of its concentration of expertise and information? Network flows may, ideally, be two-way but if one group is in a position of expertise then other groups may act as supplicants to it. Similarly with information: if one group possesses information then it may act as a gatekeeper in deciding what it wants to pass on to other groups. It can filter what it chooses to pass on. If all these are weighted in favour of one group, and particularly if that group occupies a position of centrality, then we can wonder if the relationship is reciprocal in kind. How is expertise in the processes of the ERDF acquired? In the Welsh Office, in traditional civil service fashion, training is on the job and expertise is handed down.

In the local authorities formal training is often very limited. Expertise is acquired in a variety of ways, the most common being through literature or documentation on ERDF; through examining previous submissions; through trial and error; through secondments to Brussels; through utilizing the expertise of other local authorities. Although no formal training is given by the Welsh Office the local authorities were free to contact the Welsh Office with any queries and the Welsh Office would aid them, arranging direct meetings to give guidance on particular projects. On the initial introduction of programmes the Welsh Office did run a series of seminars on filling in the new forms. Local authorities sometimes accuse the Welsh Office of gaining valuable information but failing to pass it on. The Welsh Office can alter the rules of the engagement. It consults with other government departments. The Welsh Office has greater resources at its disposal which enhance its position of centrality. For example, the Economic and Regional Policy 2 division that handles ERDF within the Welsh Office comprises approximately 30 staff who deal with project assessment, programme monitoring and any related issues such as parliamentary questions. It also deals with EC policy generally. In a small individual local authority only one or two people may be involved in ERDF as part of their work.

How was information gained? The Welsh Office received regulations and other guidance from the Commission. These were also freely available to the local authorities. Local authorities, however, lack the resources of the Welsh Office when it came to making sense of the various regulations. Thus, local authorities may be obliged to accept the Welsh Office's interpretation of regulations. The currency of a network is trust and openness and a sense of common objectives.

Access and channels of communication

Does each part of the network allow equal access or mediate for other parts of the network? How easy is it for other groups to break into the network? Networks will be characterized by the number of members, their geographical proximity to each other, the level and frequency of interactions between the members, and the strength of relations between individual members. Are channels of communication formal or informal, are decisions taken without certain parts of the network being aware of what the other parts are doing? Is there a driving hub at the centre of the network that controls it?

At an informal level individual officers in the Welsh office and local authorities communicate and have good relations. Communications take place through a number of forums:

- telephone and written contact as often as twice daily;
- office meetings where local authorities can seek help and advice;

- working groups and Monitoring Committees meet 'as necessary' and at least twice a year;
- co-ordinating committee meetings which meet six-monthly and are formal and which are attended by the representatives of the Commission.

How are these perceived by the officers concerned? The co-ordinating committees were seen as the formal conclusion to a great deal of behind-the-scenes activity. These committees were the only occasion in which all three parties concerned met formally. To some participants the committees were seen as rubber stamps and this did appear to cause resentment.

Thus we can ask how effective is access within the network itself? Not only should this question be directed at the Welsh Office–local authority relations but also at local authority–Commission relations. Some authorities do engage the Commission through secondments, use of MEPs, deputations, etc. The increased frequency of visits to the Commission by local authorities might place increased strain on the bureaucracy in Brussels. However, from 1992 the two local authority associations in Wales, along with the Welsh Development Agency, funded a dedicated service for Wales in Brussels comprising three permanent staff plus a number of secondees.

Time and resources

Time, as an organizational resource, is often overlooked but it is crucial when, as in the case of ERDF, deadlines for submissions have to be met. Time, as an organizational asset, is much undervalued and the time that a member can devote to participating in a network may determine its contribution to, and benefit from, a network. This takes on added importance when we also consider that the perceptions of time between different parties are not consistent. According to one local authority manager: 'The Welsh Office appears to think that there are large numbers of people working on EC matters in local authorities. This is not the case and it is very difficult to meet their deadlines which are often very short.'

The Welsh Office believed that the contact officers whom they dealt with in the district and borough councils spent 35 per cent of their time on ERDF matters. The contact officers themselves indicated that only 10 per cent of their time was spent on ERDF. Welsh Office estimates of the amount of time local authorities spend on ERDF were significantly different from the actual time spent. This has an impact on the time given to meet deadlines.

Similarly, perceptions of who is important and how the different members see each other and the extent of perceived importance is relevant.

Central members may be perceived to have greater potential for mobilizing resources. Not only that but a lack of organizational capacity may preclude organizations from having a greater impact on decisions concerning the distribution of ERDF. Key resources might be staffing, information and internal support.

Benefits

If it is the case that a group cannot see benefits then will it pull out of the network? Long-term considerations may override short-term disadvantages. To what extent do the different parties benefit from ERDF? In the Background Note (pp. 164–7) different concerns of the Commission and the central governments of member states are discussed as is the question of Additionality. More specifically, what do Wales and the Welsh local authorities gain from the present set-up of the ERDF? One view is that the Welsh Office role at the centre of the network does cause problems for local authorities because of its 'gatekeeper' role. But would the Welsh local authorities have benefited any more from ERDF without the Welsh Office control?

If it is the case that Wales has done well out of ERDF compared to the rest of the UK and Europe then the Welsh Office is of benefit to local authorities in Wales. Local authority managers perceived a number of advantages and disadvantages in the role of the Welsh Office:

1 Advantages:

- close contact and understanding of local problems;
- Cardiff an easier access point than London or Brussels;
- advice and information available;
- Welsh Office expertise allows smaller authorities to put together acceptable submissions;
- very good relationships with Welsh Office staff dealing directly with the operations of ERDF.

However, a number of disadvantages were also perceived;

2 Disadvantages

- local authorities are considered to be lesser partners;
- a two-way flow of information is not always forthcoming;

- the Welsh Office is not proactive in setting strategy;
- far too much information is required;
- although co-ordination does take place, the Welsh Office has its own agenda;
- good relations between staff lower down the Welsh Office and their local authority counterparts may not carry much weight on the wider Welsh Office agenda.

The benefits to local authorities have to be examined from a process point of view, i.e. does the Welsh Office role in processing ERDF help or hinder local authorities? Not only that, but the benefits also have to be examined from a contextual point of view, i.e. would the local authorities benefit from having more direct links with the Commission rather than having the Welsh Office mediate with the attendant dangers of the Welsh Office agenda forcing out the interests of local authorities in Wales? The Welsh Office view is that 'Welsh Office staff have a greater appreciation of the problems within the area. Staff feel a greater responsibility to ensure that the money is spent in Wales than a more remote authority'.

Discussion Questions

1 To what extent does the Welsh Office determine the 'rules of the game' in the allocation of ERDF in Wales?

2 How might local authorities in Wales have a greater impact on the network?

3 Does the concept of a network provide a realistic description of central–local government relations?

Background Note

The Department in the Commission that deals with ERDF is called DG XVI and comprises some 200 staff. Approximately 75 members of staff will be involved in assessing ERDF programmes. The Commission's resources have been stretched by the number of programmes to consider and their role has been that of an 'overseer'. The projects to be approved would not be examined in detail but rather to ensure that the criteria and objectives outlined in the programme would be respected. The history of the ERDF since its inception in 1975 appears to be one of tension and balance between the requirements of the Commission and the interests of the member governments. Inevitably the member governments have wanted control over the allocation of funds and some have resented and resisted attempts by the Commission to have closer dealings with sub-national tiers of government. The objective of the ERDF was to seek to limit the principal regional imbalances within the community.

More recently, the pursuit of common goals in Community operations through partnerships between the Commission, the member states and sub-national tiers of government (see Council Regulation (EEC) No. 2052/88) has been stressed. The Commission saw the ERDF as an opportunity to further a genuine supra-national European programme of action. Do the processes and criteria for funding allow this objective to be met? Prior to 1985 almost all ERDF spending was controlled by quotas which determined the proportions of the fund to be allocated to each member state. All member states received from the fund no matter how affluent. Only 5 per cent of the fund was to be distributed at the discretion of the Commission. The UK benefited to the extent of a quota of 27.76 per cent between 1975–7, 27.03 per cent between 1978–80 and 23.80 per cent between 1981–4. The UK consistently was one of the chief recipients of the ERDF. However, a consistent line taken by the Treasury is that the UK has been a net contributor to the EC and it is 'our money' anyway. The view taken by successive governments is that this money is not additional funding but should be used to reduce the amount of borrowing that a local authority might otherwise have to undertake. The quota system limited the ability of the Commission to direct development policy for Europe as a whole.

Much of the funding was distributed on an esentially *ad hoc* basis for individual projects with little chance of sustaining a co-ordinated long-term programme of investment either within or between member states. From January 1985 a system of indicative ranges was introduced which defined the minimum and maximum allocation that each member state could receive from the fund. The total minimum allocation amounted to 88 per cent of funds thus giving the Commission the opportunity to exercise discretion over 12 per cent. The proportion of ERDF assistance to individual projects was increased from 30 per cent to 50 per cent of project costs. By increasing the level of ERDF assistance it was hoped to increase competition since fewer projects could now be funded. At the same time it was recognized that the continued funding of individual projects would not enhance the more strategic role that the Commission desired in terms of a coherent European development policy. A programme approach was adopted and new types of programmes were thus introduced.

Such programmes are of three types:

1 National Programmes of Community Interest (NPCIs) which are initiated by authorities within member states;
2 Integrated Development Operations (IDOs) which involve the co-ordination of a number of different European funds such as ERDF, ESF (European Social Fund) and FEOGA (European Agricultural Guidance and Guarantee Fund);
3 Community Programmes which are initiated by the Commission and are intended to cover parts of the territory of more than one member state.

The indicative range system, the most significant part of the reforms, was intended to encourage applications from member states and by enlarging the discretion of the Commission in grant allocation to make the ERDF less of a subsidy for national regional policies and more genuinely European in its operation. And yet altering the quotas without altering the processes may not make much difference to Commission control. For example, the Commission appeared to play little part in initiating NPCIs other than determining the initial criteria. In Wales, local authorities developed their programmes in conjunction with the Welsh Office and these had to meet ERDF criteria. Indeed, counties such as Mid-Glamorgan played a leading role in setting up the initial programmes and encouraged smaller authorities to apply for European funding. It was the Welsh Office's role to scrutinize such proposals to ensure that such criteria are met. In the days of single project applications it was the Commission who decided on eligibility.

Giving the national governments the power to decide on the eligibility of projects relieved the Commission of what many within it saw as a tiresome burden of paperwork. For national governments, however, it meant a decentralization of control from Brussels to national governments. The Welsh Office quickly had in place the administrative machinery to process NPCIs. At the same time the opportunity exists for national governments to act as a sieve and filter out proposals from local authorities and any other potential project sponsors.

In drawing up applications for programmes, lack of knowledge of the eligibility criteria may deter proposals. Programmes are also difficult and expensive to devise. Those local authorities in the least prosperous regions may be the least well equipped to prepare large, long-term schemes. Thus it could be argued that, although the larger authorities may know their way around ERDF processes, without Welsh Office support smaller local authorities would not have the knowledge or experience to devise schemes that meet ERDF criteria. However, if the Commission intended the programme approach to facilitate long-term direct relationships between the Commission and sub-national government throughout Europe then it is difficult to see how this might be achieved with these processes.

In 1988, the Commission established its own list of eligible assisted areas where priority was to be given to the development and structural adjustment of underdeveloped regions (Objective 1 areas); to the conversion of regions seriously affected by industrial decline (Objective 2 areas); and to the development of rural areas (Objective 5b). In Wales, most of Gwent, South, Mid and West Glamorgans, the Llanelli Travel to Work Area (TTWA) of Dyfed, those parts of the Swansea and Aberdare TTWAs in the county of Powys, North Wales and the County of Clwyd are under Objective 2 assisted area status. The rest of Dyfed, Powys and most of the county of Gwynedd is covered by Objective 5b assisted area status. In theory, problem areas were to be defined by the Commission rather than by member states. In practice, the UK Government negotiated many of the eligible regions directly with the Commission.

The reforms place additional administrative burdens on member states, and co-operation, information and organizational capabilities from and within sub-national governments are required to assemble acceptable development programmes. At the same time sub-national groups in direct receipt of ERDF monies should, in theory, become less dependent on their central government. Following on from the move away from single projects between 1986–9 Wales received an average of 5 per cent of all the Objective 2 money allocated throughout Europe. In some local authorities the fund represented up to 40 per cent of capital expenditure.

Another factor in the attempt by the Commission to develop a coherent policy of regional development is the ambivalence towards its supra-national role by member states and by sub-national groups, particularly at the political level. If ERDF is perceived by member states as an attempt by the Commission to create some supra-national organization and therefore undermine sovereignty, then the ability of the Commission to deal directly with sub-national groups will be limited.

10

Local Authority Decision Making: The Traders of the Uffizi Gallery in Florence

Chiara Narcisi

Florence is a town in the centre of Italy with a population of about 400,000 inhabitants. It stands on the river Arno in the eastern part of a valley surrounded by mountains. It is an historic town having the highest concentration of works of art in Europe. Tourism is one of its most important industries. Small and medium-size firms are mainly involved in metallurgy, chemical or mechanical engineering or involved in the production of consumer goods such as cigarettes, cloth, clothes, shoes. Craft factories (pottery, laces, furniture) are characteristic of the town, perpetuating a very old tradition.

Florence local authority has a council of 60 members. The 'majority' that supports the *Giunta* (see Glossary Appendix 10.2) is a coalition of five parties: Christian Democratic Party, Socialist Party, Social Democratic Party, Liberal Party and Republican Party. The PDS (the ex-communist party), the Greens and the MSI (Italian Social Movement) make up the opposition. Therefore the *Giunta* is made up of this five-party coalition (*pentapartito*) that has also been the central government coalition for many years. The mayor belongs to the Socialist Party. See Appendix 10.1 for background information on the Italian system of local government.

This case examines the decision–making process in local government. It illustrates the relationship between different levels of government and indicates the multiplicity of different stakeholders who have an interest in what at first appears to be a minor issue. The case demonstrates the difficulties of making and implementing decisions within tight deadlines.

The Case of the Traders under the Uffizi Gallery in Florence

Florence is defined as a *città d'arte* (city of art) since it has the highest concentration of works of art in Europe. Therefore the tourist and commercial activities depending on it are an extremely important resource for the economy of the city. Any observer coming to Florence can easily realize how the town centre – full of souvenir shops, snack-bars and standard-menu restaurants – is organized for the thousands of tourists that any year – from March to October – pour into the city. The size of the town centre is very limited and the narrow streets, with the massive buildings located one after the other, make it very difficult to find further areas for new commercial activities. Not only that but the local administration has been unable to do any substantial planning for the relocation of the traders who sell their goods on stalls located near some of the most important artistic and architectural sites in the city. The economic interest of the traders has always been considered extremely important, perhaps more important than the conservation and protection of the historical and cultural assets.

A good example of this are the traders who were selling their goods under the Gallery of the Uffizi, one of the most important museums in Italy. Permission had been given to them at the beginning of the 1950s by the mayor of the city who wanted to give jobs to unemployed citizens while gathering together all the souvenir stalls spread around the town centre. From that time the number of the sellers increased gradually until, by 1992, the gallery of the museum was entirely occupied by 23 stalls.

Many complaints came from different groups (central and local administrators, superintendents, directors of the museum, citizens and historians of art) but the administration of the *Comune*, always very careful in protecting the interests of trade in the city, had never been able to deal with the demands of the traders. However, a decree, promulgated on 24 March 1993 from the national *Ministro dei beni culturali e ambientali* (Minister for cultural and the enviromental assets) ordered the removal of 23 traders from the gallery of the Uffizi. The Minister had been pressed into taking this measure by the two *Soprintendenti*, civil servants responsible for the protection of historical and artistic assets and for the protection of architectural and environmental assets in the area. National law declares that in these cases the local administration has to find a new site for the traders.

The Decision-making Process: a New Location for the Traders after the Decree of the Minister

As soon as the decree was issued the traders began to protest and reacted negatively to the decision of the Minister. 'It's an unfair measure', said the president of one of the associations representing the interests of the traders. 'It's unjust that such an important decision is taken from on high without any bargaining and without doing any planning to find different alternatives for the traders. The decree of the Minister is completely ill-timed with this increasing economic crisis and it shows how the State is able to be strong just with the weakest people.'

'The tourist season is going to start', said one of the traders of the gallery. 'We work seven days per week selling the merchandise we bought in the winter. So at this time in the year our stores are full of stuff and our wallets are just full of debts! If we have to move elsewhere we will really run risks to our business.'

'We can't go away right now!' said another trader. 'The local administration must delay until the end of October the implementation of the decree. In this way we can pass the tourist season and modify our stores, putting a cover over them. We really can't run the risk of going outdoors with uncovered stalls without the protection of the gallery. Even Ferdinando I of the Medici, prince of Florence at the end of the XVI century, before sending away the butchers from Ponte Vecchio to substitute them with the goldsmiths, gave a delay and found them an appropriate place. So the Minister will be surely more democratic than the old lord of Florence.'

The traders also complained about the motivations behind the decree. 'It's not true that we ruin the gallery selling our souvenirs under it!' claimed a press release published – at the expense of the traders – in a local newspaper. 'If we weren't under the gallery it would be much more ruined. From the morning until the evening we are the wardens of the gallery and protect it against vandals and drug-addicts. We clean the basement at the entrance of the museum every day and also give information to the tourists performing social tasks that the local authority is not able to carry on. Nobody has the right to send us away, especially the bureaucracy that has been neglecting the place for such a long time.'

The union representative of the traders was particulary angry with the decision of the Minister 'They have been trying to evict us without succeeding since 1962 and they will not suceed this time. Not only that, but there is a law which allows the central government to move the sellers away from the places of architectural and artistic interest just if the *Comune* is able to find them an equally rewarding location'. However, this interpretation of the law is misleading. The law allows the traders to carry on their business elsewhere but there is no mention of the economic rewards of the new location.

The traders and their representatives tried to get a suspension of the decree from the Minister. They wrote informal letters (to the Minister, and to the local authority) and appealed to the regional tribunal against the decree. These tactics, however, did not succeed. The Minister was adamant: 'It is a measure that has needed to be taken for a very long time. The souvenir stalls under the Uffizi Gallery are an eyesore and are damaging. They are an obstacle to the full enjoyment of the light and the perspective that history has handed down over the centuries. So my decision guarantees the public's right of appreciation of that monumental area and it is thus irrevocable.'

The same position was assumed by the two superintendents who had pressed the Minister to send the traders away from the gallery. The superintendents are appointees of the central administration and depend on the Minister for the Environment even though they have a high degree of autonomy in performing their tasks. The superintendent for environmental and architectural assets in particular was fully committed to assuring the implementation of the decree by the local authority. He fixed 30 April as the date by which the gallery was to be free from the traders: 'There is a decree that has to be implemented, if the traders don't leave the area by the end of April I will request the intervention of the police.'

The reaction of the local administrators to the decree of the Minister was ambiguous. They tended to support it but at the same time wanted to avoid the protest of the traders, specifying that the decision had been taken by the Minister and that the local authority could not do anything but implement it. From their point of view the *Comune* had the task of finding a new acceptable place for the traders. This task involved, in particular, the *assessore* for trade. 'The decree did not catch us completely unaware', the *assessore* said. 'We expected something like this and have already prepared some feasible solutions that will be proposed to the traders soon. First of all, however, I must see the officers of my department and define the proposals that will be presented to the *Giunta* and the mayor.'

The administrators of the trade department of the local authority put foward three possible solutions for the sellers; two of them were immediately feasible, the third one could be implemented in the long term.

Solution 1. Piazza Castellani

The first solution was to place the stalls of the sellers in Piazza Castellani, a square located behind the Uffizi, exactly on the other side of the building. The advantage of this placing was its closeness to the former location of the sellers; nevertheless the area was partially occupied by a building yard set up for the enlargement of the museum. The work on the reorganization of the museum had been in progress for some years but had been interrupted because of funding problems and irregularities in the management of the works.

Solution 2: Piazza dei Giudici

The second proposal was to settle the sellers in Piazza dei Giudici, a small square that was also quite close to the Uffizi Gallery (about 100 metres away), but located in a more isolated position, further from the usual tourist routes. This location was strongly opposed by the sellers since they considered it unprofitable.

Solution 3: Piazza Repubblica

The third possible alternative was Piazza Repubblica, a large square built in the nineteenth century close to the main street of the city. In this square the traders could find a permanent settlement constituting a stable souvenir market. The square however was not immediately available. Piazza Repubblica was not closed to the traffic at that time and, besides its pedestrianization, two existing parking lots (one for taxis and another for the residents of the square) would have had to be removed. It would, therefore, be necessary to commission an architect to draw up a detailed plan for the reorganization of the square.

The *assessore* of trade thought the best alternative was the first one, since Piazza Castellani was very close to the museum and could offer good opportunities for the traders. This alternative was then approved by the *Giunta* and presented to the traders at the end of April. In the meantime the mayor and the Government had reached an agreement that the date for the implementation of the decree could be delayed until 31 May and the mayor committed the local authority to the removal of the unfinished works in the builders yard at the Piazza Castellani.

Nevertheless the reactions of the traders were very negative: 'Piazza Castellani is offensive to us', said one of the traders. 'It is occupied by a building yard and is out of the tourist routes. We will move there just when the works of the Uffizi will be finished and the exit of the museum will be placed in Piazza Castellani.' Other traders were equally scathing: 'Yes we are ready to move, but the local administration has to find an equally rewarding location', said a representative. 'We propose Piazza della Signoria, (which is the main square of Florence, where the town hall is, and faces on to the Uffizi Gallery) otherwise the local authority could give us the permission to sell our merchandise inside the museum itself.'

The solution of Piazza Castellani was opposed by two permanent commissions within the council. The trade and the culture commissions, when asked to examine the proposal of the *Giunta* before it was discussed by the council, rejected it. 'The proposal doesn't give a definitive solution to the problem,' argued the president of the culture commission. 'Piazza Castellani will be surely degraded by the stores of the traders. The *Giunta* should modify its proposal, increase the alternatives and plan for a real tourist market in the city.'

When the proposal was discussed by the Council on 21 May 1993 no general agreement had been reached.

The First Decision of the Council

The meeting of the council was introduced by the mayor:

Today the assembly has to decide about the destination of the traders since the decree of the Minister forces them to leave the Uffizi gallery. It's a decision taken by the Minister and we can't do anything to change it. The local authority must just implement it, finding a new place for the traders according to the law. The superintendent for the envirnomental and architectural assets fixed by the end of May the deadline for the implementation of the decree and he is not going to delay it anymore. It is crucial then that the Council makes a decision today. We can't take the responsibility to send the traders away without finding a place for them. The *Giunta* carried out a long technical and political preliminary investigation. The administrators of the Trade department identified three possible solutions which have been discussed with the sellers.

I think that Piazza Castellani is the most feasible of the three. The square is very close to the museum and the superintendent has already given his agreement about it. Nevertheless I'm ready to accept the second alternative (Piazza dei Giudici) as well, if there is the general agreement of the Council, even though I think Piazza Castellani is the best one. What we must do is to take a decision anyway.

The *assessore* of trade agrees with the mayor:

> Piazza Castellani is the best solution of the three the *Giunta* put foward. It has the advantage of being very near to the Gallery offering good economic opportunities for the traders. If we choose another site that is further from the museum we run the risk of considerably reducing these opportunities. By the way it's going to be a temporary solution that will be reviewed when the works for the enlargement of the museum start again.

The *assessore* for the Culture agrees:

> It's not a measure to punish the traders. We are aware of the services they offer to the tourists as well as of the importance of their activities for the economy of the city. The decision to remove them from the Gallery is included in a wider plan for the reorganization of the squares in the city. I agree with the *assessore* of trade: Piazza Castellani seems to me the most feasible location since it was approved by the superintendent and doesn't cause many poblems because of the traffic.

Nevertheless many councillors disagree with the choice of Piazza Castellani for different reasons.

'I totally disagree with the choice of Piazza Castellani', argued the other superintendent (for the artistic and historical assets) who was also a member of the town council:

> If we settle the souvenir market in Piazza Castellani we will definitely hinder the plan for the reorganization and the enlargement of the museum. Now the works are at a standstill because of funding problems but it's likely they'll never start again if we place the traders where the building yard stands now. The solution is not convenient even for the traders who would be placed in a small and untidy area partially occupied by a building yard. I propose the second alternative; Piazza dei Giudici can be a very appropriate place for the traders even though not so near to the museum it might become the square of the 'small market' where the tourists will go on purpose just to buy the souvenirs. Nevertheless I think that the council should ask the Minister for a delay of a couple of months just to reorganize the square for the market.

Another councillor, who was also the president of an association representing the interests of the traders, was in complete disagreement with the proposal of the *Giunta*, but for entirely different reasons:

The decision of the Minister has been taken without any regard for the traders since it ignores the interests of the people who have invested in their activities. The tourist season is going to start, so sending the traders away from the gallery might cause them serious trouble. What about the traders who have just spent a lot of money investing in this new activity? What about those who have got into debt during the winter, hoping to pay them with the income from the tourist season? The Gallery can't be considered just a work of art, we can't ignore that it's also a place for commercial activities. Not only that, but we can't take any decision from on high, as the Minister did, we must negotiate it with the traders. Piazza Castellani is unacceptable since it's occupied by a building yard; Piazza dei Giudici is too far from the museum and away from the traditional tourist routes. I propose via dei Gondi instead, it's the street that, from the Uffizi goes to the Church of Santa Croce and all the tourists, after visiting the museum, pass from there to go and visit one of the most famous churches in the city.

The proposal is also opposed by a green councillor:

Piazza Castellani is an improvised solution that is not up to the city. It might be accepted only as a temporary alternative to gain time to implement a definitive solution. The green group proposed the third alternative the *giunta* had put foward. The traders could find a final location in Piazza Repubblica and it could be, at the same time, a good occasion to resettle and pedestrianize the square. Thus my group is going to present an amendment to the proposal of the *Giunta*. It commits the local authority to put foward a plan for the reorganization of Piazza Repubblica.

'No I can't accept this', said the mayor. 'We can't commit the administration to lay down a plan that could be implemented only after a very long time. Piazza della Repubblica can be just a consideration for the future, not a committment for the *Giunta*.'

The amendment was rejected by the council as were rejected two proposals – presented by the groups representing the parties PDS (Democratic Party of the left, the ex-communist Party) and MSI (the Italian Social Movement) – asking the Minister for a delay to the implementation of the decree.

The decision

The proposal of the *Giunta* was not approved or rejected as the council was split: 18 councillors voted for the proposal and other 18 against it.

When the superintendent of the environmental and architectural assets knew the council hadn't taken any decision, he became very angry:

> I reached an agreement with the mayor and delayed to May 31st the date for the implementation of the decree. The delay was just to give him the time to move the building yard from Piazza Castellani and make some room for the traders. Now it seems the local authority doesn't want to fulfill the agreement; well the term has been definitely fixed and I'm not going to give any other delay. The traders must leave the gallery by the end of the month otherwise I'll call the police to set it free.

However a solution was found by the council three days later. It emerged from a compromise between two different exigencies: to find a site for the traders in a very short time, and to plan a better and more stable location in the longer term. Piazza Castellani was chosen as a temporary solution, but the local administration committed itself to put foward a plan for the definitive settlement of the stores in Piazza Repubblica. Unfortunately this solution, achieved after a lot of bargains, could not be implemented. On 27 May the area set aside for the traders was exploded by a terrorist attack that shocked the world. Therefore the traders had to leave Piazza Castellani where they had already settled and some of their stores and merchandise was damaged. The explosion was during the night, but some of the sellers were keeping their goods in stocks close to the museum.

After the attack the Minister for the cultural and enviromental assets promulgated another decree forbidding any trade in the area around the museum. So the mayor and the *Giunta* had to look for another place for the traders.

Another Place for the Sellers, a Second Decision of the Council

The local administrators were very upset by the new decree. 'It's an irresponsible decision', said the mayor:

> The Minister seems to ignore all the difficulties we have faced just to find a new location for the traders that could be accepted by the majority of the council and the traders themselves; Piazza Castellani was, in fact, the only immediately feasible solution. Not only that but I can't find any positive support for the decree.

Everybody in Florence agreed with the decision of freeing the gallery of the museum from the stalls; now, however, the citizens are supporting those who have lost their jobs because of the explosion. I think it's a duty of the city to give the traders a place to work; in such difficult circumstances for the city nobody can ignore the interests of trade. I've written a letter to the Minister in which I express my disagreement with his decision, I hope it will have an influence on him otherwise the *Giunta* might appeal to the regional tribunal against the decree.

Most of the *assessori*, like the mayor, openly criticized the decision of the Minister who forbade the location of the sellers in Piazza Castellani.
'That decree is ridiculous', argued the *assessore* for the town planning.

The decision of the Minister reopens the question of the traders and increases their claims for a profitable location. I hope he will change his mind otherwise it is going to be very hard for the local authority to balance the general interest with the private one. I agree with the mayor it's likely we will appeal to the regional tribunal against the decree if the Minister doesn't cancel the ban in Piazza Castellani.

Piazza Castellani is definitely the best solution, the *assessore* for Culture pointed out. 'It's not true that the stores invade the security area, we have already set out a plan to locate the traders at a comparable distance from the museum'.
The Minister, however, did not modify his decision and the local authority had to find another location for the traders.
The traders themselves, who had never accepted the solution of Piazza Castellani since the beginning, raised their claims after the terrorist attack. 'I have lost part of the merchandise because of the explosion', said one of the them. 'The local authority must find a profitable location for us so that we can recover our losses during the summer. Via dei Gondi can definitely be an appropriate solution. This street, that goes from the Uffizi Museum to the Church of Santa Croce, is always full of tourists who pass this way to reach one of the most famous churches in the world'.
'We want to settle in Piazza Repubblica straight away', said a representative of the traders. 'The location has already been decided by the town council, but it was delayed to give the administrators enough time to plan the reorganization of the square; in this emergency situation however, we want authorization to go to the square now, in time for the tourist season'.

The Third Decision

On 15 June the *Giunta* approves a proposal of the *assessore* for trade: the souvenir market will be temporarily placed in Piazza dei Giudici, but an architect of the *Comune* is invited to draw up a plan for the resettlement of Piazza Repubblica within 90 days. The proposal is presented to the town council three days later.

'Piazza dei Giudici is the only immediately feasible solution', said the mayor, who introduced the council meeting:

> I have disliked this alternative myself and have preferred Piazza Castellani in the last town council meeting, but now, after the decision of the Minister that forbids any business in the area of the museum, there isn't any other possible solution to implement in the short term. Anyway it's just a temporary solution. By the end of September the plan for Piazza Repubblica will be ready and the traders will move to a much more profitable location. Until then the local administration is committed to put signs indicating the placing of the market all around the town centre.

This position is shared by the *assessore* of trade who set out the proposal and by the superintendent for the historical and artistic assets who had been supporting the alternative of Piazza dei Giudici since the beginning. The proposal, opposed by many councillors (in particular the president of the traders association and the president of the commission for culture), is approved by the council with just one majority vote.

The traders who were present at the meeting reacted immediately, occupying the council chamber. The tension was high for a few days. 'Piazza dei Giudici is too far from the tourist routes. We won't be able to make any business there. The mayor himself – in the town hall meeting of 21 May – opposed this alternative saying it was dangerous because of the traffic and not profitable at all; you can listen to his words!' said one of the traders taking a tape recorder with the recording of the mayor's speech.

On 29 June most of the traders started a hunger strike and conducted a sit-in in front of the town hall to demonstrate against the choice of Piazza dei Giudici. 'We will move from here just by an ambulance!' the trade union representative exclaimed.

Two other representative associations of the traders disassociated themselves from the protest.

'When I saw the traders on hunger strike I felt very embarassed and upset,' said the president of one of the traders association. 'This strategy is going to be completely ineffective and the traders run the risk of compromising their bargaining power in front of the local administration'. On the 7 July, after more than one week of hunger strike, some of the traders burst into the council chamber and fought with some of the councillors and two policemen who were brought in.

The mayor and the *Giunta* condemned the reaction of the traders and decided to interrupt the negotiations using strong-arm measures. They called the police to take the traders away and make them finish the hunger strike. From that time the negotiations with the local administrators were carried on only by the representatives of the traders associations who dissociated themselves from any extreme lobbying strategy.

The tension decreased during the summer; some traders moved to Piazza dei Giudici while some others did not, preferring to wait for the reorganization of Piazza Repubblica.

On 7 September 1993 the *Giunta* approved a first plan to reorganize Piazza Repubblica and entrusted a team (made up of officers belonging to different departments) to produce a draft of the executive project. None the less the new location for the traders caused others problems and was opposed by different interests.

In the Piazza Repubblica there was only enough space for 18 of the 23 traders. The traders' representative associations decided to work in shifts of four days per week since the local authority did not find a place for the five stores left in the area around Piazza Repubblica. However, other interest groups complained about the decision of the *Giunta*.

'We haven't anything against the traders,' said the owner of a hotel in the square, 'but we fear the pedestrianization of Piazza Repubblica. How can the tourist buses get into the square to bring the tourists to our hotels? Some travel agencies are already threatening to cancel the hotels of Piazza Repubblica from their list.'

The residents of the square complained because the local authority (to leave enough room to the tourist market) had deprived them of some reserved parkings. 'The administrators have taken off 59 parking places and now we have just 29', complained one of the residents.

'We can't go on like that', said a member of a committee for the safeguarding of the town centre. 'The administration doesn't do any planning for the town centre and any decision is taken to solve single problems and satisfy particular interests. The historical centre of the town should be considered like a quarter of the city, not just like a place to make business with the tourists!' Some conflicts emerged among the local administrators within the *Giunta*.

'I voted against the decision of the *Giunta*', argued the *assessore* for the economic development. 'The *Giunta* has decided too quickly under the pressure of a lobby. The placing of the stores in Piazza Repubblica is profitable just for a small minority and damages the other economic operators and the residents of the square.'

'I've voted for the deliberation of the *Giunta* just because I wanted the reorganization of the square', said the *assessore* for the traffic, 'but I'm against the settlement of the souvenir market. Piazza Repubblica is wonderful without any trafic and the traders would be an element of disorder. I propose a city referendum to make the citizens decide about the location of the traders.'

The mayor and the majority of the *Giunta* did not take into account these views. The traders settled in the square the 21 September and the local administration went on implementing the decisions taken in the deliberation of 7 September.

Discussion Questions

1   What are the problems that the local administration is asked to solve in the decision-making process?

2   Who are the most important actors in the decision-making process? What are their interests, What the strategies and the solutions proposed?

3   Which interests had to be balanced by the local authority?

4   How can a very small interest group, almost insignificant in its electoral influence, have such an impact on the local administration and on public opinion?

Appendix 10.1: General Information about Italian Local Authorities

The Italian territory is divided into three levels of local administration: the *regioni* (regions), the *province* (provinces) and the *comuni* (communes), the smallest level of local administration. Italy is divided into 20 regions with legislative powers in certain fields and having extensive administrative powers. In any region there are provinces with few administrative competences that co-ordinate the largest level of local government (the regions) with the smallest: the communes. Italian communes are traditionally important institutions in representing the political and the social interests of the local community and have done so since the Middle Ages. The importance of these local authorities within a tradition of self-government is also demonstrated by the large number (more than 8,000) of them spread in the whole territory. Most of the communes are very small in size with more than half having a population with less than 3,000 inhabitants.

Internal Organization of the *Comuni*

The *comuni* have important administrative powers even though they cannot produce any legislation. These powers are fixed by laws according to some general principles of decentralization set by the constitution. Any *comune* has three organs of government: 1) the *Consiglio* (council); 2) the *Giunta* (junta or cabinet); 3) the *Sindaco* (mayor).

1   The council is the representative assembly of the local community. It is directly elected and has a variable number of members depending on the population of the *comune* (the number of the councillors goes from a minimum of 15 members for the *comunes* with a population smaller than 3,000 inhabitants, to a maximum of 80 members for the ones with a population exceeding 500,000 inhabitants).

The council (being representative of the local community) is a political organ frequently divided between different groups corresponding to political parties most of which are represented in Parliament. Within the council it is possible to find – in the largest communes – permanent commissions specialized in certain fields of local government. For example, in the case study, the culture and trade commissions are key stakeholders.

The council has a competence to perform a limited number of crucial acts specified by law. These acts concern decisions regarding the internal organization and the external activities of the local authority. All the other acts not explicit reserved to the council are performed by the *Giunta* or by the bureaucracy of the local authority. The council elects the *Giunta* and the mayor. Reform of the electoral system was approved in March 1993 by the Italian parliament. The mayor is now directly elected, together with the council.

2   The *Giunta* is an executive body much smaller than the council. It may
    have a minimum of four members for the *comune* with a population
    smaller than 3,000 inhabitants, to a maximum of 16 members in the
    comune exceding 500,000 inhabitants. Its members, called *assessori*, are
    usually members of the council but also ordinary citizens chosen for
    their specific technical skills.
       The *Giunta* has a general administrative competence in performing all
    the acts not explicitly attributed to other organs by the law. Its role is
    to propose policy and oversee the council's implementation of its gen-
    eral political goals. Any *assessore* is mainly interested in a specific field
    and is in charge of an *assessorato*, an administrative department cor-
    responding (in the bureucratic organization of the *comune*) to a *settore
    funzionale* (functional sector). In the *comune* of Florence for example
    there are *assessori* for: health care, education, culture, budget, etc. Their
    activities can be decided by the mayor, the *Giunta* or the council ac-
    cording to the statute of any local authority.

3   The mayor plays a fundamental role in the local administration. He or
    she performs the following tasks in:

    • representing the *comune* to other organs or institutions;
    • convening and chairing the town council meetings;
    • supervising the local bureaucracy and checking the implementation
      of the Acts delegated to the *comune* by the central government or by
      the regions;
    • performing any other function attributed to him or her by the law,
      the statute and the internal regulations of the local authority.

    Moreover the mayor has the powers of a public officer in fulfilling some
    tasks (all specified by the law) concerning public security, public order,
    elections, military service, etc.

The Bureaucracy of the Local Authority

Any *comune* has its own bureaucracy. While national politics sets general
criteria for the organization of local bureaucracies, this legislation is sufficiently open to give the *comuni* significant autonomy in structuring the
internal organization of their administration. Florentine bureaucracy is

organized into different departments (*settori funzionali*) corresponding to the different administrative tasks performed by the *comune*. In Florence there are, for example, departments concerning public care, environmental issues, education, culture, trade and markets, etc. These functional sectors are divided into *unità funzionali* (functional units) having specific competences in the field. For example the trade and markets sector is divided into unit corresponding to specific fields of specialization, e.g. permanent trade and itinerant trade; permissions to do various trading activities, etc.

Any sector is managed by an executive. At the top of this bureaucracy there is a secretary (*segretario comunale*) who is the most important local officer. His or her tasks are: to give technical/ administrative consultation to the representative organs; to write down a record of the council meetings; to co-ordinate and monitor the organizational structure of the local authority.

Appendix 10.2: Glossary

Assessore/i   members of the local *Giunta*, the executive body of the local authority

Assessorato/i   departments of local administration run by the *assessori* of the *Giunta*

Comune   commune, smallest level of local government in Italy

Consigliere/i   councillors, members of the *Consiglio comunale*

Consiglio comunale   town council, the assembly of the *comune*, directly elected by the local community.

Ministro dei beni culturali e ambientali   minister of the cultural and environmental assets

Provincia   province, second level (in size) of local administration

Regione   region, biggest level of local government

Sindaco   mayor, first citizen elected (under the old electoral system) by the town council

Soprintendenti   superintendents, civil servants, appointed by the *Ministro dei beni culturali e ambientali*, responsible for the protection of the historical and artistic assets in the area

11

Capital Accounting Case Study – UK Local Government

GEOFF JONES

This case is designed to illustrate a number of themes surrounding the introduction of a major change in UK local government accounting practice. Most elements of the change were first implemented in most local authorities for published accounts for the financial year 1994/5. This qualification of the extent of implementation highlights the major theme of the case: that significant changes of accounting practice are not simply a question of expert professionals devising a single, 'best' practice and accountants and managers applying them unproblematically. Although standardization of accounting practices has long been pursued as an aim of the accounting profession, encouraged or perhaps driven by certain interested users of financial information such as governments and providers of capital, diversity remains a key feature of all types of accounting activity.

Accounting professionals tend nowadays not to see accounting numbers as representing *the* truth about an organization's financial state of affairs but rather a particular version of the truth which coincides with the accounting conventions which governed the preparation of the accounts. Audit certificates under UK Companies Acts require the auditor to confirm their opinion that the accounts under audit represent a true and fair view of the financial affairs of the company. Thus there are two important qualifications to the truth of the accounts: the auditor's *opinion* that they are true (auditors can be wrong), and that truth is in some way inextricably linked with *fairness*, which in this context implies some kind of comprehensive, non-selective representation of accounting facts. In the UK public sector, the wording 'presents fairly' is used. So it is recognized that the same accounting 'facts' can result in significantly different sets of accounts.

The duty of the accountant, generally speaking, is to prepare accounts in accordance with the accepted conventions *and* to disclose in what ways and to what extent these conventions have not been complied with. This implies that there may either be difficulties in drawing up the accounts of an organization in compliance with the accounting conventions (for example, arising from the specified information being unavailable or too expensive to collect), or that producers of accounts may prefer one particular method of presentation to another (especially regarding the organization's assets and liabilities). Although accounting conventions (largely but not entirely codified as national and international accounting standards and 'Generally Accepted Accounting Principles' (GAAP)) attempt in principle to minimize scope for diversity, there are so many variables affecting an organization's financial standing (e.g. the industry and country in which its major activities take place, its recent and prospective profitability, its strategic intentions regarding major investments, merger or acquisition activity, the nature of its audit profession) that there remain many ways of representing its 'real' position. Consequently interpretation of accounting information has become a highly skilled activity practised by analysts of various kinds, usually with an eye to the interests of their corporate customers, e.g. the financial institutions.

Two interesting issues which have preoccupied the accounting community (i.e. including both producers and users of accounts) in recent years have been how to account for the value of so-called intellectual property (patents, software, performance rights, etc.) and for the value of company brand names. These are obviously not the only or even the most important emerging issues to have been tackled, but they have some similarities as accounting problems with the governmental accounting issue discussed in this case, namely that of accounting for the substantial capital assets owned and operated by UK local governments.

These similarities revolve around perceptions and definitions of the issue (i.e. how an issue becomes an issue), how the regulatory bodies search for and decide on a 'solution', and how (whether) the 'solution' is actually implemented as intended. Although these processes are played out differently, with different actors and concerns, nevertheless these three stages can be discerned in the case which follows, even though stages 1 and 2 occurred several times but stage 3 only once in the 125 years covered by the case.

The main point to bear in mind here is that commercial accounting has problematic issues of its own which it finds difficult to address despite the proliferation of apparently self-regulating yet prescriptive accounting bodies and institutions throughout the world. Accounting is not simply a question of applying agreed and autonomous rules to any given situation.

Most importantly for this case, it is not just a question of applying 'good commercial accounting practice' to governmental institutions, even though there may seem to be good prima-facie reasons for trying to do so.

Even 'fundamental' accounting concepts were introduced into different industries and organizations at different times and in different degrees, and although there may have been something of a convergence in the last 50 years or so (perhaps due to the concentration of ownership of capital in particular countries such as the US and the subsequent export of that capital into US-controlled businesses throughout the world), new issues and problems continue to preoccupy accounting regulators and practitioners. Accountants tend to regard changes in accounting practice as developmental, i.e. progressive in the sense that accounting today is better than accounting in the past. Many researchers, however, look on accounting in much the same way as they do any other social practice, i.e. that these practices somehow are more reflective of the society which produced them and are therefore the result of a 'negotiated order' rather than the outcome of an objective search for new techniques and methods which better represent some underlying reality. Both parties acknowledge that there is no one set of permanent, objective, context-free 'laws' of accounting which apply to all conceivable circumstances. But they sometimes differ in their evaluation of the practices in use.

This case tells us a lot not only about UK local government but also about other parts of the UK public sector and possibly about the ways professionals of all kinds seek to retain their autonomy by owning and solving problems relevant to their practice area. Part of the impetus for the changes that were considered and adopted for local government arose out of successful application of new capital accounting regimes, first in the water industry and more recently in the National Health Service in the UK. Central government departments are preparing to introduce a similar regime for all UK state expenditure which will be completed early in the next century. So the example of local government may be seen as representing a much wider set of changes.

Objectives of the Case

This case has the following objectives:

- to illustrate the processes by which an important change in local government accounting in the UK came about;

- to highlight the roles played by different interests and stakeholder groups in these processes;
- to explore the different meanings that are given to accounting conventions.

Capital Accounting – the Arguments

Conventional accounting seeks to show the value of assets, usually based on their historic cost, with some recognition that most assets wear out, become obsolescent, etc. Depreciation is the accounting means of measuring and recording this depletion of value, and there are various ways of estimating the reduction in value which can be said to arise in a particular accounting period. For example, it is possible to depreciate an asset over its useful life so that at the end of the period it has no value and is written out of the balance sheet, or to provide depreciation so that at the end of its life enough depreciation has been provided so as to replace the asset at its then market price. The varying pace at which an asset's value declines can be accommodated, e.g. we are familiar with the idea that a new car loses a large percentage of its value as soon as it leaves the showroom yet declines in value more slowly thereafter. Some assets can appreciate in value: land, for instance, and in these cases capital reserves are created. Still others, for example railway tracks, will maintain their value so long as adequate repair and maintenance is carried out. Hence it may not then be appropriate to depreciate them. Despite sometimes heated debate, the historical cost convention is still the most widely used in all kinds of accounting: current or replacement cost bases, though used, are not so widespread.

From the mid nineteenth century to the introduction of the new capital accounting regime in 1994/5 local authority assets were shown in accounts in a way which emphasized the remaining amount owed on them rather than what they cost, let alone what their value was estimated to be. This was because other sources of finance, for example contributions from local income (such as markets and tolls), local authority trading undertakings (e.g. gasworks), or from rates, were extensively (and legally) used. Although there was usually great enthusiasm from reforming councillors to provide the new amenities the public were said to need, in the interests of prudence authorities frequently repaid debt early. After repaying the loan, no further charge for using the asset appeared in the revenue accounts. For those authorities which exceeded their minimum disclosure requirements set down by the Local Government Board and which did show the historic cost of their assets (mainly county boroughs, metropolitan boroughs and joint trading boards, i.e. the main urban areas of the country) the undepreciated historic cost of the asset remained in the balance sheet and could remain there forever. For other authorities, only the loans outstanding were shown. It was the variety of practices in use, the emphasis on loans rather than economic cost and the pressure from the mainstream commercial accounting bodies which led to capital accounting becoming a big issue in the 1980s.

The Issues

Local Authority balance sheets portray councils as debt-ridden. They do not get anywhere near showing their true worth. Revenue accounts are downright whimsical in their portrayal of the cost of assets used up in providing services. The remarkable thing is that after a century of local government, that state of affairs should still exist. (John Scotford, County Treasurer Hampshire County Council and Chairman of the CIPFA Capital Accounting Working Group, *Public Finance and Accountancy*, 19 February 1993, p. 12)

For any professional body to be worth the name, it has to be concerned with raising standards, including advocating new standards when old ones have served their time. What is acceptable in one circumstance may become quite unacceptable in another. (Noel Hepworth, Director of CIPFA, *Public Finance and Accountancy*, 19 February 1993, p. 2)

In a Utopian world the concept of asset rental would underpin all accounts in both the public and private sector . . . [W]e do not live in such a paradise, but rather in a mean spirited, anti-public sector environment. Acceptance of theoretical virtue of the nebulous aspiration does not provide a basis for extrapolating that into a mandate to impose an expensively irrelevant system of accounting on local authorities. (Jeff Pipe, Assistant City Treasurer, Birmingham City Council, *Public Finance and Accountancy*, 19 February 1993, p. 20)

These quotations identify two important aspects of the 'problem' of capital accounting in local authorities in the UK in the late 1980s. These issues relate primarily to local authorities in mainland Britain. Some local authority accounting terms, conventions and regulatory arrangements are different in Scotland from those in use in England and Wales. These differences do not affect the substance of this case. One aspect is historical: reforms, by definition, must have something to reform: no reformer starts with a blank sheet of paper and hopes to implement changes unhindered by the past (see Appendix 11.1 for details). The second is the concept of interests in accounting: professional practitioners, for instance, have interests, probably in raising standards but also perhaps in retaining or enhancing their social position, which raising standards helps them to do. The implications of both these aspects as espoused by the practitioners themselves in these quotations are that accounting is not one fixed body of knowledge applicable for all time, and that changes to it may not necessarily be brought about simply because some experts see deficiencies which *could* be remedied.

The Decisive Period 1980–1990

The oil crisis of 1973 is claimed as the turning point, but it seems likely that sooner or later some fundamental shock to the UK economy was bound to occur. The first budgets of the Labour Government elected in 1974 saw the official demise of Keynesian demand management and the beginnings of the turn to monetarism under the inflation/stagnation combination that affected many Western governments, but the balance of payments crisis of 1976/7 and the IMF loan terms to restrain public expenditure set in train the first round of local government budget pressures which have continued ever since.

Perhaps as the result of some combination of professional ambition and fiscal crisis, this period was also the beginning of the revival of interest in local authority capital accounting. In 1975 CIPFA's Accounting Panel published a pamphlet on Local Authority Accounting which proposed, *inter alia*, that capital assets should be depreciated if revenue costs were to be correctly stated. As part of its attempts to accede to the mainstream of UK accountancy, CIPFA was also reviewing the applicability to local authorities of a wide range of accounting standards and proposed standards, and another working party recommended (in 1977) a system of notional loan charges (to be called capital charges) to attempt to reflect the true economic costs of using assets in the revenue accounts of local authorities.

Following the logic of the practice of emphasizing the amount owed on assets in the balance sheet, the 1972 Local Government Act had laid down specific requirements for pooling and charging the debt repayments to revenue accounts, and the changes proposed would have necessitated some revision or accommodation of this which would have been difficult and/or expensive to implement. But the main obstacle was the uncertainty about the way the accounting profession in general would deal with the problem of asset values following the period of high inflation in the UK economy.

So-called Current Cost Accounting (CCA), which attempts to recognize the effects of inflation on company assets and performance, proved a minefield for all parts of the profession and, despite years of controversy, proposals and counter-proposals, no effective standardized accounting regime emerged, although some UK companies did, and continue to, produce current cost accounts.

The height of this uncertainty occurred in the late 1970s and early 1980s, and the proposals for reforming capital accounting were delayed pending some resolution. CIPFA felt obliged to show its commitment to CCA by recommending the adoption of current cost accounts for local authority trading activities. Enthusiasm for 'proper accounting' was again a strong force in the new Thatcher Government in the personality of Michael Heseltine in charge of the Department of the Environment and a strong prevailing feeling throughout the government that local authorities were overlarge and inefficient, and were contributing to the unnecessarily high interest rates the new monetarist outlook emphasized. The Department of Trade and Industry under Lord Young and others continued to signal the desirability of a unified UK accountancy profession.

One of the Thatcher Government's earliest pieces of local government legislation, the Local Government Planning and Land Act 1980, introduced the obligation for local authority Direct Labour Organizations (DLOs) – the parts of local authorities which existed to carry out approved local authority work such as refuse collection and highways maintenance – to expose themselves to competition with the private sector through the competitive tendering process. And here the issue of the value of local authority assets compared to their accounting treatment comes into focus, for the Act required DLOs to prepare their accounts (and hence their bids for contracts) on a current cost basis and to achieve a required rate of return on their assets valued at current cost (current cost here meaning current replacement cost – the highest basis for valuation and one which was not widely used by the private sector competitors for contracts). The general effect of this in accounting terms is to increase the prices which must be charged in order to maintain the current cost of assets while at the same time apparently depressing profitability because income is lower in relation to the highly valued asset base. This effect was one of the reasons it proved widely unpopular with companies at large.

But local authorities were encouraged to continue to find ways of extending the applicability of commercial accounting practices. However, many argued that the concept of depreciation, for example, entailed a conception of capital maintenance which was inappropriate for many local authority assets and, more importantly, could not form the basis of a charge to ratepayers.

Instead, a system of asset rents was proposed which could form the basis of a charge to operating departments for the use of assets but which would not be related to rates. In other words, the discipline of charging for use of assets would not affect the level of rates being charged – an important clarification of principle which had always been one of the key problems of reforming the accounting system, the separation of external reporting arrangements which would always need to show debt outstanding (yet was otherwise more or less incomprehensible to the non-accountant) from the fiscal pressure to make services like education do more with less.

The Audit Commission

The establishment of the Local Government Audit Commission for England and Wales in 1984 provided a further impetus to the reform of local authority accounting practices, bringing as it did a much wider involvement of private sector audit firms into local authority audit than existed under the previous 'approved auditor' system. Additionally, the Commission took seriously its role in promoting 'best accounting practice' in local authorities and one of its major initiatives was the development of a Code of Practice for Local Authority Accounts (1987) which took the accounting profession's Statements of Standard Accounting Practice and reconsidered the extent of their applicability to local governments. This code effectively became binding on local authorities since it redefined the meaning of the 'proper accounting practices' they were obliged to pursue.

One important part of accounting practice was left out of the Accounting Code: capital asset accounting was left on one side as 'too difficult' and would have significantly held up the introduction of the rest of it. But the Minister's (by then Nicholas Ridley) quoted response ('This is all very well but what about capital?') drove home the significance the Government attached to the issue. As before, the local authority accounting profession were left under the threat that if it failed to find an acceptable solution to the need to update its 'antiquated' conventions, the Department would impose its own solution. Whether it could ever have done this remains open to question; suffice it to say that not only was it a challenge to CIPFA's claim to be a self-regulating professional body, but many of its members believed that anything it could devise would be better than a scheme dreamt up and imposed by the civil servants. This possibility was repeatedly used later by the Institute's leadership as a means to deter sceptical opinion.

The Role of the Capital Accounting Steering Group

Whether real or imaginary, this threat, and the general embarrassment that the years of discussion had produced no workable proposals, led to a determined effort to resolve the issue once and for all. A high-profile Capital Accounting Steering Group (CASG) was set up on 1 January 1988 under the chairmanship of John Parkes, then Director of Finance of Humberside County Council and a CIPFA council member. The local authority associations (i.e. non-accountants) were represented as it was essential that non-finance Chief Officers and Councillors would not be automatically alienated from the Group's findings. The DoE, the Audit Commission, Scottish local authorities and academia also supplied members. Secretarial support (and guidance) was provided by CIPFA and Price Waterhouse provided technical support, e.g. in advising on commercial practice and in testing out some of the possibilities for change.

The CASG spent a year deliberating and finally came forward with a set of proposals for consultation in February 1989. These embodied many of the features previously favoured. A charge for assets in use was to be made in the service revenue accounts based on their current value (defined as net current replacement cost, i.e. current replacement cost after accumulated depreciation) plus a charge to reflect the cost of capital (i.e. the opportunity cost of tying up capital in its current use). The balance sheet would show assets at depreciated current replacement cost or market value. Assets would be grouped into four main types:

1 council dwellings;
2 other land and buildings;
3 infrastructure;
4 vehicles, plant, furniture and equipment.

The benefits of this arrangement were that it brings the economic cost of holding assets to bear on the service manager using them and at the same time allowed balance sheets to show 'proper' valuations without requiring additional funds from ratepayers (soon to be Community Charge payers).

The consultation period ended on 15 January 1990 – a lengthy gap, but in the meantime several authorities were to act as pilot sites for testing the practicability of the proposals, the biggest immediate problem being the drawing up of full asset registers. At the publication of the proposals (February 1989) the new system was envisaged as being implemented in the financial year 1991/2, i.e. beginning just after the close of the consultations.

The Response of the Professionals

The results of the consultations graphically illustrated the underlying tensions among the CIPFA membership and elsewhere. The perception of the leadership that the Institute needed to maintain its claim to be a 'proper' accounting body and retain its power of self-regulation in the face of governmental threats cut little ice with many of the membership who would have to implement the new proposals. The consultation document came at a difficult time (although it was argued that there had never been an easy time to make such changes). Following many years of legislative and structural changes in local government, and continued fiscal pressures, the government's sweeping reform of local taxation – the community charge or poll tax – was about to be introduced, the main feature of which was the transfer of the basis of assessment and charging of local tax from property (as it had been since time immemorial) to individuals on the grounds that it was they who actually consumed so many of the modern services which local government provided. Apart from the political controversy which surrounded its introduction, the logistical and practical difficulties of identifying, assessing and billing a new and wider range of local taxpayers in the time scale prescribed by Government fell heavily on CIPFA members. The problems inherent in adopting the proposed new system of capital accounting were widely seen as unnecessary in themselves and impractical to implement.

This type of response drew attention to one of the ambiguities in the situation. The stated intent of the CASG was to produce proposals which separated the capital cost of services from their financing, showed the full current costs of services and recorded the current value of fixed assets. This rather glossed over the important distinction between the external reporting requirements of local authorities (which the Code of Practice on Local Authority Accounting was concerned with and which, as we have seen, had excluded capital accounting) and the different issue of how efficiently authorities used the assets under their control. The DoE and the rest of the accounting profession, although interested in both, were primarily concerned with external reporting, mainly on the grounds that, in the DoE's case, it was still the formal accounts that provided the main basis for financial control of local authority expenditure and debt and, in the case of the accounting profession, from its assumption that internal efficiency depended on 'proper' accounting, meaning to them accountability to shareholders and stock markets.

CIPFA members, however, showed great scepticism about many of these assumptions. Something like 80 per cent of responses (including corporate bodies and non-accountant organizations) contained criticisms of the proposals. In general, they were unimpressed by suggestions that meeting DoE requirements was the same thing as improved accountability to rate and charge payers. Many felt the public were already well served by the financial information available to them. An alternative heresy put forward was that nobody bothered to look at local authority accounts anyway and that balance sheets, for example, simply did not have the same significance in the public as in the private sector since it was not part of the role of local authorities and other public bodies to aim primarily at increasing their net worth. Thus the internal disciplines were actually more important and many of the presumed benefits of this could be achieved by exhortation and comparative studies (as performed, for example, by the Audit Commission) rather than by a full-blown accounting system which might come to be regarded as just another accountants' wheeze unrelated to the 'real' concerns of managers. A surprisingly large volume of opinion seemed to regard many aspects of accounting as less important than delivering services. And some members implied that CIPFA should be finding better things to do than impose extra burdens on its members at the behest of the Government and the other accounting bodies.

The Role of CIPFA

This kind of response threatened the credibility of the leadership and the full weight of its disciplinary power was brought into play. The 'Why change?' kind of criticism was met with emphatic statements about how the imperfections of the current system had long been recognized and no longer proved adequate in the new competitive and constrained environment local authorities were now in. The 'Why now' kind of response was met with emphasizing the threat to self-regulation, supported by the evidence that during the consultation period the government had apparently considered the CASG report and imposed a similar system of capital charges in the NHS from the financial year 1990/91. It was easier to do this in the NHS since most of its accounting still used the cash basis and there were no loan accounts, but the implementation problems were simply brushed aside and a charge to services was introduced based on depreciation on all assets valued over £1,000 (an absurdly low figure – later raised to £5,000 – which spoke volumes for the outlook of the civil servants who devised it) and a charge to equate to a cost of capital. After years of deliberation by CIPFA, this single step by the Department of Health greatly added to the urgency of finding an acceptable solution for local government, and incidentally undermined many of the objections that the valuation task in local government would take an impossibly long time to get right.

Also at this time relations with the rest of the accounting bodies were further sensitized by the failure of a major merger attempt in 1990. This time, with the shrinkage of its public sector base and a worsening of its financial situation (though with a small but definite growth in active members) the long-term future of the Institute became less secure and prompted a rash of strategic and marketing initiatives designed to support an indefinite independent existence but still within the main professional regulatory bodies.

So the suggestion that the published accounts of local authorities were comparatively unimportant brought the most scathing response, expressed more moderately much later when the final revised proposals were adopted:

> The Institute as a professional accountancy body is committed to upholding professional accounting standards. The Institute cannot be seen to endorse a system which results in a completely meaningless financial statement, when that statement, the balance sheet, ought to be of major significance – as it is elsewhere in the economy.
> So there is no justification for the argument that no change should be made.
> (Hepworth, *Public Finance and Accountancy*, 19 February 1993; p. 2)

But other objections proved more difficult to brush off. In particular, the costs of implementing the new system and the proposed time scale were seen as at best unnecessarily high and short. Complaints about the asset registers prompted the response that authorities would need to know what they owned anyway, either for competitive tendering purposes or simply for good housekeeping. As such, the costs could not be regarded as wholly additional. The Royal Institution of Chartered Surveyors which had been involved in the proposals offered advice on how to simplify and accelerate the valuation process, including the use of information then available as a result of the revaluing of businesses that took place at the time of the community charge introduction.

Implementation

Another line of criticism was that market valuations rather than current replacement cost could be the only basis for a 'real' economic cost, but the non-marketability of many local authority assets (e.g. roads and schools) made this difficult, although research was done at some of the pilot authorities to see how far this idea could be taken. The pilot studies, however, also threw up problems of their own. The involvement of other professional groups in endorsing and implementing the proposals was more difficult at grass-roots level than the attitude of the national bodies seemed to imply. Cost in particular was an issue, and later in the implementation phase some councils let it be known that their finance department would be expected to shoulder the additional financial burden. But problems associated with the assets themselves were unearthed. For instance, valuing roads proved even more difficult than had been envisaged since it turned out that for the purposes of depreciation a road had many different components which wore out at different rates, for example the wearing surface had a short life compared to the substructure. Was each of these components to be valued and depreciated separately?

All these reactions caused severe difficulties to the CASG and the Institute. Reaction was so unfavourable that despite producing a 'final report' in September 1990, the CASG recognized the difficulties and deferred the implementation of its proposals while yet more studies were carried out under yet another working group, whose remit was to find ways in which the new system could be implemented relatively simply and at minimum cost to local authorities. This time the pilot authorities were Solihull Metropolitan District Council, St Edmundsbury District Council and the London Borough of Croydon and this time the DoE was persuaded to finance the studies. Another 'interim' report was produced (on 8 May 1992) with the significant amendment to the earlier proposals that, subject to certain caveats relating to an authority's policy to maintain the economic life of the building by making adequate provision for repairs and maintenance and to depreciate if this were not the case, operational buildings and other properties should not be depreciated but included at current value (as previously defined).

This change was proposed 'primarily as a pragmatic response to the practical concerns expressed by commentators on the [CASG's] Final Report' (*Public Finance and Accountancy*, 8 May 1992, p. 10). The other main problem, council houses, were also to be valued on this basis, rather than on their value to their tenants under the 'right to buy' legislation (which was substantially lower). Finally, valuations were to be simplified by using a 'beacon' system where only one of a type in a neighbourhood would be valued. Infrastructure and so-called 'community assets' (parks, historic buildings, etc.) valuations would be based on historical cost and so would not need current valuations. The RICS was an important source of legitimation for these steps. The interim report of 8 May 1992 also reported that a survey had been carried out to see whether the new system was thought to be workable and in particular that it would be consistent with or unaffected by proposed changes by the DoE to the system of capital expenditure controls.

The interim report for the first time proposed implementation of the revised proposals for 1994/5 accounts, i.e. four years after the initial expectation of the CASG in 1988. Even then, the required approval by CIPFA Council was not entirely smooth with one council member voting against. A strong statement stressing 'professionalism' and 'proper standards' was made by the CIPFA Director (second quote under 'The Issues') to the membership following the adoption of the proposals on 29 January 1993 and an Institute Statement was issued. This stressed the 'limited room for manoeuvre', the 'full exploration of the options', the necessity of 'a degree of compromise and pragmatism', the need to recognize developments in other parts of the public sector, and finally that 'the proposals represent the best balance between action, pragmatism and principles'.

Further consultations were carried out, but the battle was essentially won (or lost, depending on your viewpoint). The revised proposals were incorporated into a revised Accounting Code of Practice for local authorities and became the Statement of Recommended Practice in 1993. One Treasurer wrote in PFA: 'the mood of practitioners I meet is one of mild acceptance, certainly not wild enthusiasm . . . there is general acquiescence.' (*Public Finance and Accountancy*, PFA 9 July 1993 p.13). Many authorities were slow to get their asset registers set up and help was at hand from a wide array of valuers, software suppliers, private accounting firms and management consultants who were all able to benefit.

It remains to be seen whether the benefits in terms of accountability and better use of assets are actually realized (and how this is assessed), but it is clear that the main objective of being able to deliver a 'proper' accounting system for local authorities had at long last been achieved.

Discussion Questions

1   Who were the key stakeholders, and what were their interests, detailed in the case?

2   How appropriate are commercial accounting practices for the public
    sector?

3   What is the value of public assets and who should decide this?

4   What does the case pinpoint as the key issues facing public sector
    professionals?

Appendix 11.1: The History of Local Government Capital Accounting

There is no doubt that perception of capital accounting in local authorities
as a 'problem' dates back in several important respects at least to the adoption of the system of accounting which prevailed for well over a century:
the emphasis in local authority accounts from the mid nineteenth century
onwards not on the value (current or historical) of the assets owned by local
governments but on the amount borrowed to produce them.

The conventions which were imposed by central government on local
authority accounting in the nineteenth century through the Local Government Board (created in 1871 through a merger of the Poor Law Board and
the medical department of the Privy Council), together with the involvement of the Board of Trade and the Treasury (a triumvirate of departmental interests which was to remain crucial to local government down the
years) could be said to embody the dominant values of the time within
a workable regime. A feature of this regime was the pre-eminence of governmental administrative perceptions and requirements (represented by
the Treasury and the Local Government Board) rather than accounting
interests as represented through the Board of Trade and by the embryonic
accounting profession. This perception emphasized the separate legal status of local authorities and their liability in respect of loans taken out by
them, but also an apprehension over the size of the rising national debt and
the need to ensure that local authorities behaved responsibly with the
rapidly rising funds provided directly by ratepayers and indirectly by taxpayers through government grant-in-aid. Thus the departments sought to
control the variables important to them through the legal and administrative methods they were familiar with rather than through the accounting
regimes which shareholders and accountants had instilled into commercial
concerns.

One consequence of this was an emphasis on cash accounting which has
persisted up to the present day. For a long time, under an Act of 1882,

authorities were required to keep accounts on a 'receipts and expenditure' basis – a misunderstanding by Parliament which was the subject of some derision from both local authority and 'commercial' accountants as it demonstrates clearly the lack of appreciation of accounting niceties of which the profession complained. It was generally accepted that what was meant was 'receipts and payments', i.e. the cash accounting convention rather than the 'income and expenditure' basis favoured by the accounting profession. The latter involves a recognition that events with financial consequences could have occurred but not yet affected the organization's cash flow – for example, goods having been received but not paid for by the end of the accounting period.

These 'accruals' remain one of the basic accounting conventions, even in public services (but not yet in all central government departments). A further aspect of the accruals convention is another non-cash charge on the accounts which is vitally implicated in the debate about capital assets: depreciation. A full accruals basis implies that the cost of asset depreciation is also recorded in the accounts even though no cash is involved. This was one of the main problems with introducing full accruals into local authority accounts which defeated a number of initiatives over the years.

The effect of all this was that, even on an historic cost basis, accounts did not clearly show the value and cost in use of the assets owned and operated by local authorities and, for instance, made it impossible to show the growing lobby of ratepayers concerned about the massive increase in rates which occurred during the nineteenth and early twentieth century that their money was being wisely spent on lasting assets rather than, as many suspected, being used to support municipal profligacy and to encourage idleness among the recipients of services.

Detailed accounting requirements were an intrinsic but only one part of the whole regulatory regime imposed by the Local Government Board and its successors. For large capital projects this included the granting of a private Act of Parliament to proceed, a loan sanction to borrow the monies required and a stipulation of the maximum period of the loan. This maximum period was intended to ensure that authorities did not owe money on assets which had decayed. Consequently they were set for periods not expected to exceed the useful life of the asset. Although originally the maximum period for the repayment of loans used for acquiring land was set at 120 years, this was quickly brought more into line with the life of the assets built on it, and a maximum of 60 years came into effect. It was later argued that the loan repayment was essentially the same as depreciation, since it corresponded to the depletion in value of the asset as the loan was redeemed. However, a range of issues including fluctuating interest rates, technological changes (e.g. the widespread use of gas and electricity), and variations in the use of loan finance meant that this correspondence was only approximate, although it almost certainly distorted values less than the historic cost convention itself.

By the end of the nineteenth century most municipal corporations had extended their activities into a wide range of undertakings including water supply, gasworks, electricity supply, tramways and canals. Some of these enterprises were new but some were acquired from private sector owners. The issue of appropriate compensation sparked a long-running debate about the accounting conventions of local authorities compared with those of their private sector equivalents. As with other developments, municipal corporations obtained the power to acquire or establish these trading undertakings by local Act of Parliament and with it the sanction to borrow the necessary funds. As with other assets, the balance sheets of the local authorities gave few clues to their current market value. However, since at this time the justification for these undertakings was the provision of public services, the question of their book value which would be needed for subsequent sale simply did not arise. It was thought (by the Local Government Board and the Treasury) to be far more relevant to concentrate on the extent of government indebtedness, hence capital accounts typically began with the entry 'loans outstanding – Town Hall'.

Other interests had rather different concerns. Private owners of utilities which were municipalized were interested in obtaining the maximum price they could, although here as elsewhere their accounts were unlikely to provide a basis for a transfer value, since valuation and depreciation practices varied widely and owners were anxious to stress the potential as well as the historic value of their assets. Privately, some owners were only too glad to get rid of decaying assets, such as obsolete water mains or old tram tracks, at a large profit, and the political tide to put these 'essential services' under public control meant that even otherwise shrewd councillor–businessmen were happy to go along with recommendations from their officers to acquire the patchwork of privately provided services to knit into the municipal fabric.

There were also, however, discordant voices. Political opposition to municipalization objected not only to the process itself (and the powers the corporations had secured for themselves) but also to the financial regime to which the municipal enterprises were subject. The latter not only involved increasing the national debt but also the presumed inefficient financial administration which would arise under municipal ownership and give rise to additional local taxation. These views became part of a strong lobby to bring 'proper accounting practices' to bear on local authorities and for them to be audited by trained, qualified accountants rather than the long-established system of audit which consisted of lay members of the community elected annually to inspect the accounts. These auditors tended to be either lawyers or worthy laymen; it was argued by the accounting lobby and its allies that they were hopelessly ill-equipped to pass judgement on the probity of complex corporation accounts which, moreover, included activities which had often been taken over from the private sector where they had been subject to private sector accounting disciplines.

This campaign was only partially successful and in a way which also demonstrates the relative power of government departments rather than the accounting profession: despite hostility from the municipal corporations, the audit eventually came under the control the Local Government Board itself and became the District Audit, but it developed its own specialized workforce which did not employ trained accountants in a big way until the 1960s. At the turn of the century the district auditors' insistence on cash accounts, reflecting the government's interests, was one of the sources of local treasures' antipathy towards them.

A potent force in the lobby for more 'professional accounting' was the ICAEW, who in a long series of articles in the *Accountant* in the 1890s and elsewhere drew repeated attention to the deficiencies as they saw them of municipal accounts. This culminated in a series of articles entitled 'The form of municipal accounts' in 1897. Praising Sheffield Corporation for showing its assets at historic cost less depreciation where appropriate, i.e. in accordance with commercial conventions (this was additional to the requirements of the Local Government Board), it took the opportunity to attack Bolton Corporation whose Treasurer was at the time president of the Institute of Corporate Treasurers and Accountants (formed in 1885 and later becoming the Institute of Treasurers and Accountants and, eventually (IPFA)). But his balance sheets clearly demonstrated the local accountants' rationale for the predominant form of local authority accounts. He had three headings for his capital assets:

1 'Remunerative and Realizable Works', which included gasworks, electric supply, waterworks, markets and tramways, i.e. municipal trading undertakings;
2 'Unremunerative but Realizable Works', which included the town hall, parks, recreation grounds, museums, cemeteries ('less grave spaces sold'), depots, etc;
3 'Unremunerative and Unrealizable Works', including street improvements, sewage works, roads and a bridge.

202 GEOFF JONES

The valuation basis of each of these classes of asset is revealing: the first two classes are stated at cost less sinking fund provision (a method comparable to depreciation whereby amounts are set aside as investments which eventually provide funds for the replacement of assets). The final class, however, is treated as being worth only 'the amount from time to time due upon them', i.e. the balance of loans outstanding. The logic for this, in the perspective of the time, is understandable, although criticized by the *Accountant*: since there was no thought or intention to sell things like roads and sewers and no alternative to local government being responsible for them, it follows that their most definite determinable value is the amount of any liability owing on them. This logic underlies the whole debate about asset valuation of governmental assets and is only really challenged when the idea of transferring assets from public to private control (or vice versa) is raised. It is not quite as straightforward as this, however: proposals for nationalization or privatization also revive or reflect interest either in the alleged inefficiencies and poor financial control of public bodies (as a critique of nationalization) or their alleged inadequate accounting procedures (as an obstacle to privatization). In both cases, 'proper accounting' is one of the remedies offered.

What perhaps is most remarkable is the durability of the administrative regime imposed by the Local Government Board throughout a period where its validity was frequently challenged by a range of different and often powerful interests. This in turn raises the question of what was different about the forces and arguments deployed in the late 1980s and early 1990s which eventually succeeded in changing it.

The Post-war Period

This issue again became prominent in the immediate post Second World War period when a wide variety of industries were nationalized. The new nationalized industries frequently consisted of both private companies and former municipal undertakings and again the question of compensation assumed prominence and again the differences in accounting practice were crucial. In the electricity industry, for example, compensation to private companies was contested and said by their owners to be unfairly low, but the terms on which municipal electricity undertakings were to be taken under central government control provoked an outcry from local authorities and their ratepayers. Compensation was offered on the basis of 'net debt', i.e. the amount outstanding on the loan used to provide the asset. The paradox was that not only did the net debt basis not reflect the current and future value of these usually profit-making entities, but the more prudent a council had been in building up that enterprise through being more reluctant to borrow and perhaps relying on higher contributions from the rates, etc., the lower their compensation was to be. Some 370 municipal electricity undertakings on which an aggregate of £400 million of capital monies had been spent were to be nationalized for a capital sum of about £200 million, while the capital sum payable to about 190 company undertakings with assets at cost of some £300 million were to be nationalized at something more than that. In the gas industry it was estimated that the market value of the assets was £91 million yet the outstanding debt on which compensation was to be paid was only £22 million. Needless to say, the net debt basis for the transfer of municipal assets prevailed.

The Role of the Accounting Profession

It is often argued that the post-war nationalizations represented some kind of high-water mark for collective aspirations and consensus in the UK whatever assessment is made of the subsequent performance of these industries and whether or not they achieved the hopes of the originators. This consensus more or less prevailed for over 30 years. Although there were always comments about the control of local spending and the extent of central government support of the rates, on the whole public expectations of public services continued to rise and Labour and Conservative governments vied with each other to build more roads or houses. Meanwhile, the accountancy profession was busy extending its membership and influence. Municipal accountants were no different, and throughout the 1940s and 1950s tried repeatedly to obtain a Royal Charter for their Institute. This was finally granted in 1959 with the appearance of a deal whereby district auditors, by then employees of the Ministry of Housing and Local Government, were able to become members, i.e. recognized as qualified accountants, a status which had previously been denied them. Later, auditors from the Government's Exchequer and Audit department were also allowed to join.

The structural reforms of local government put in place by the Heath administration (1970–74) spread municipal accountants widely beyond local government with the establishment of new separate entities for health, water, gas, electricity, transport and urban development. Seeing this as an opportunity to break out of the municipal corral, and following a failure to merge with the ICAEW in 1970, the IMTA obtained a supplementary Royal Charter, becoming the Chartered Institute of Public Finance and

GEOFF JONES

Accountancy in 1973, and began to seek a stronger voice on the governing committees of the accounting profession. Influenced by its new proximity to the mainstream of accounting views, a continuing perception that a unified profession could achieve more than its component bodies alone and by pressure from the new Department of the Environment, the CIPFA leadership began to encourage discussions about 'improvements' to accounting and reporting practice based on the application of commercial accounting conventions, such as Accounting Standards, into public authorities.

Municipal accounting practice during the 1960s and 1970s had concentrated on the new possibilities opened up by statistical techniques, for instance in resource allocation decisions, and the computers to run them. Inter-authority comparisons became easier to perform and highlighted the huge range of accounting and reporting practices in use. Internally, great emphasis was placed on integrated structures and new management techniques, largely imported from America, such as PPBS and MBO. The new county councils and metropolitan authorities were heralded as being the evangelists for a new scientism and rationality in local government affairs. Local government professionals like lawyers and valuers began to be ousted by a new profession in local government — managers. And treasurers and accountants were their natural allies.

Glossary

ADC   The Association of District Councils
ACC   The Association of County Councils
AMA   The Association of Metropolitan Authorities
ASC   Accounting Standards Committee (now Accounting Standards Board – ASB)
CIPFA   The Chartered Institute of Public Finance and Accountancy
DoE   Department of the Environment
DTI   Department of Trade and Industry
ICAEW   Institute of Chartered Accountants of England and Wales
MBO   Managing by Objectives
PPBS   Planning, Programming and Budgeting System

Notes

Public Finance and Accountancy, 8 May 1992, p. 10.
Public Finance and Accountancy, 19 February 1993, pp. 2, 12, 20.
Public Finance and Accountancy, 19 July 1993, p. 13.

Index

accountability, 6, 41, 67, 75, 81, 85, 96, 103
agencies, 74, 75, 82, 85
  see also Next Step Agencies
Audit Commission, 190, 193
autonomy, 97, 160

case studies, 1–6, 32, 57, 73, 90, 104, 123, 158, 168, 184, 186
centralization, 96
Citizen's Charter, 13, 124, 128, 130
community care, 135, 136, 138
  funding, 125, 136–7, 141
  health authority role, 127
  local authority role, 124
  housing department, 128
  private sector, 126
  users and carers, 127
  voluntary sector, 126
Consultative Committees (police), 105, 111
contracts, 67
  contract management, 139, 156
  contract specifications, 126, 129, 134, 146
  contracting out, 93, 125, 139
cost centres
  education, 34
  local government, 58–63, 139
culture, 61, 63, 78, 79, 83, 86, 90, 91, 93, 97, 99, 100, 104, 108, 110, 130, 132
Customer Charter, 58

Decentralization and Devolution, 65, 69, 70, 73–7, 86–8, 131
departments, 74, 75, 77, 79–82, 84, 86, 88
Direct Labour Organizations (DLOs), 190

Education Reform Act (1988), 42–3, 51–2, 88–9
efficiency unit, 15
enabling authority, 57–8, 61, 124, 130, 136, 139
European Regional Development Fund, (ERDF), 158
  European Commission, 164, 165
  funding, 164, 165
  local authorities, 159–66
  training, 160
  Welsh Office, 159–61, 163, 166

federal government, 71
Financial Management Initiative, 6
further education
  central government, 42, 49
  colleges, 32, 49, 77, 78
  competition, 38, 39, 46, 48, 50
  culture, 36
  franchising, 33, 43, 47, 48
  incorporation, 34, 35, 43, 47–9
  management skills, 35, 36
  mission statement, 37
  professionals, 50
  quality, 38, 49

Silver Book, 35, 36
strategy, 37, 38, 40
Further Education Funding Council
(FEFC), 33, 38, 39, 45–7
Further and Higher Education Act (1993),
50–1

Generally Accepted Accounting Principles
(GAAP), 185

Health and Safety Act (1974), 44

implementation, 65, 82, 123
Italian local government
background, 180, 183
bureaucracy, 182–3
council, 168, 173, 175–6, 178
glossary of terms, 183
relations with central government,
170–1, 176–7

Joint planning, 86, 128, 131, 138, 140
see also Networks and Partnerships

Local Education Authority (LEA), 32, 34,
38–9, 42, 47, 74, 78–9, 81, 89
Local Government
business units, 69
commercial activity, 60, 68
devolved responsibility, 59, 62, 65, 68
finance, 64–5, 68
information systems, 64, 65
performance management, 61
politician-manager, 62, 64, 65
professionals, 61, 63
service users, 66, 69
structural change, 65
targets, 60, 64, 66
Local Government Act (1972), 189
Local Government Act (1988), 42, 44
Local Government Commission, 86
Local Government Planning and Land Act
(1980), 190

management
by objectives, 112
change, 101

competences, 20, 83, 87
controls, 104
development, 83
styles, 84, 102
managing contracts, 129
market principles, 130
mergers, 90, 92, 100
mission statement, 31, 97, 107, 154

National Association of Teachers in
Further and Higher Education
(NATFHE), 41, 48
National Health Service (NHS)
district health authorities, 154
GPs, 153, 154
internal market, 152
needs, 151
Patient's Charter, 130, 151, 154
patient satisfaction, 152
professionals, 150, 151, 153
quality of health, 152
Trusts, 149, 151, 153, 154
National Health Service and Community
Care Act (1990), 135, 154
networking, 63, 66, 80, 81, 151, 157–8,
161–3
Next Steps Agencies
accountability, 6, 9, 13, 14, 16
block allocation system, 7–8
Chief Executive, 6, 8, 9, 11–16, 20, 22,
25, 28
efficiency, 12, 22, 30
Framework Document, 8, 9, 11, 14, 23
market testing, 12
ministers, 25
objectives, 9–11, 18
organizational structures, 8, 24
pay, 18, 19, 28
performance, 6, 11, 13, 17, 23, 25,
26–7
staff activities, 21
Treasury, 11
workload forecasting, 13–14

objectives, 67, 99, 100
see also Next Steps Agencies
organizational change, 57, 68

partnerships, 57, 60, 63, 65, 68, 79
performance, 66, 75, 149, 150
permanent secretaries, 14, 15, 28–9
personnel, 6, 13, 15, 16–19, 28–30
prefect, 80, 82
professionals, 63, 82–3, 97, 127, 139, 184,
    189, 193–4, 196, 203
Public Accounts Committee, 15
Public Expenditure Survey (PES), 12,
    112
purchaser-provider relations, 74, 87,
    124, 127, 132, 136, 140, 147, 151,
    154

regional aid, 160
regional policy, 158, 166
responsiveness, 76

Service Level Agreements, 61
Special Transitional Grant, 141
stakeholders, 5, 13, 41, 98–9, 101, 125–6,
    129, 152, 158, 168
Standard Spending Assessment, 128
strategy
    in education, 37–40, 46, 48, 76
    in local government, 58, 65, 67–8, 129
strategic change, 57, 62, 64

targets, 60, 66
trade unions, 90, 92, 94, 115
Training and Enterprise Council (TEC),
    38, 43, 45–8, 77

welfare pluralism, 136
Widdicombe Committee (1986), 83

Printed and bound by CPI Group (UK) Ltd, Croydon, CR0 4YY

09/06/2025

14686103-0005